complete the doodle

Doodling is a way to unwind and relax, but sometimes the hardest part is getting going on a good piece of mindless art.

Use the following pages as a starting point. Combine them into a drawing, draw something greater, go beyond the lines and the pages, and even color and scrapbook the pages into oblivion. Do as you please, use this book in any way that helps your mind and body take a breather from every day life.

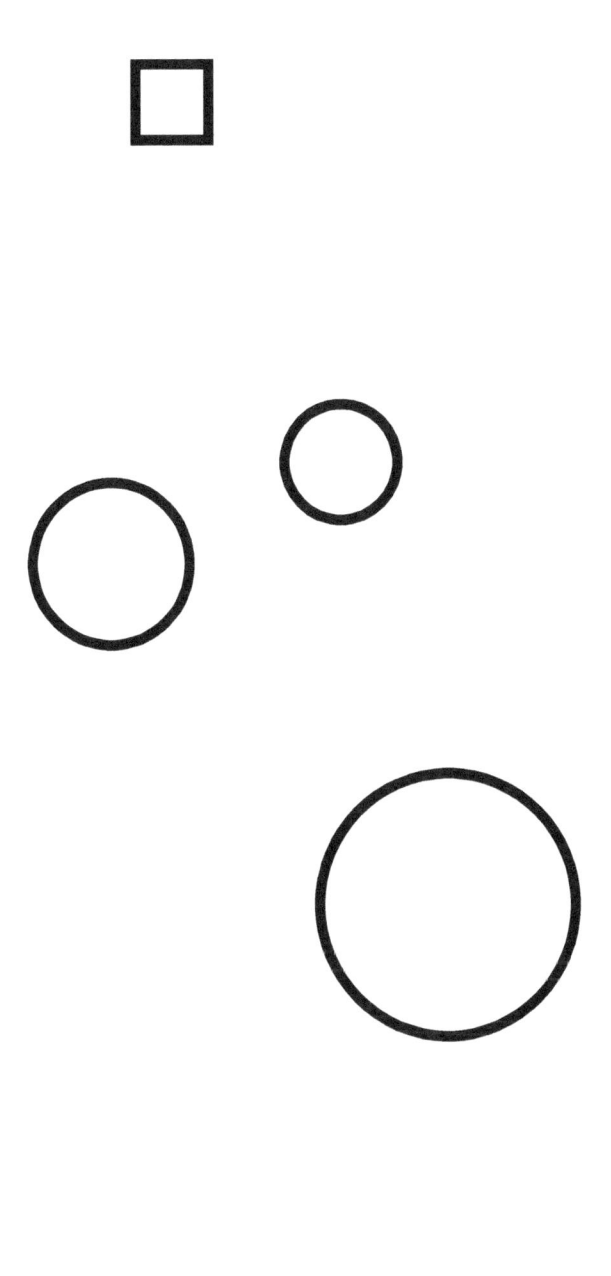

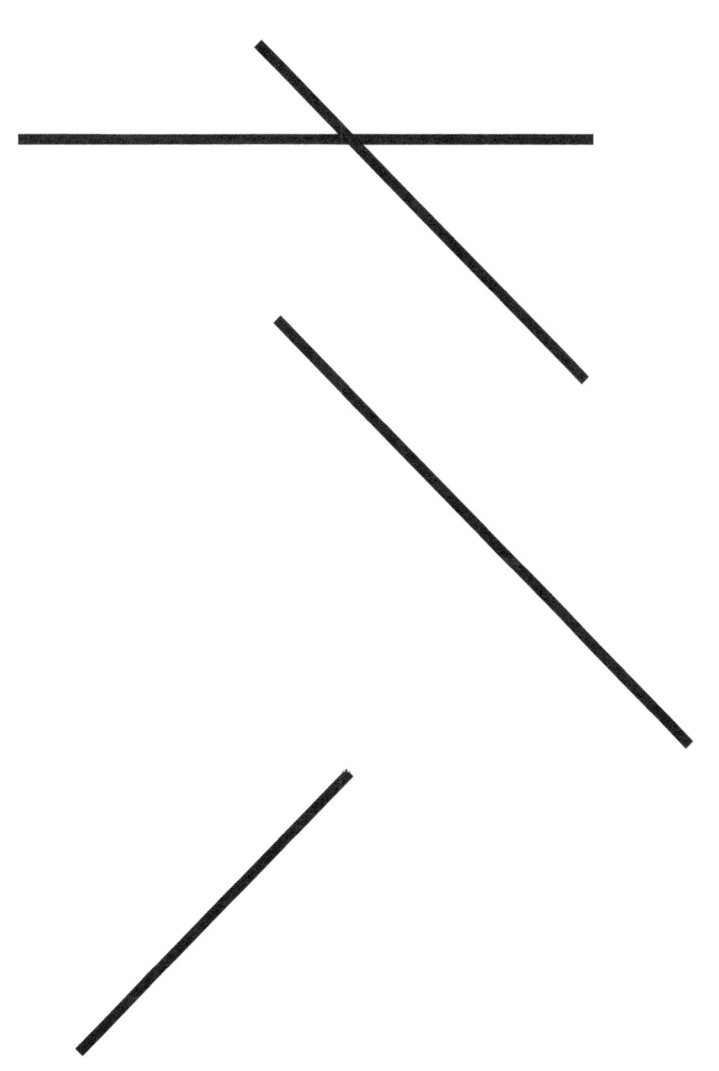

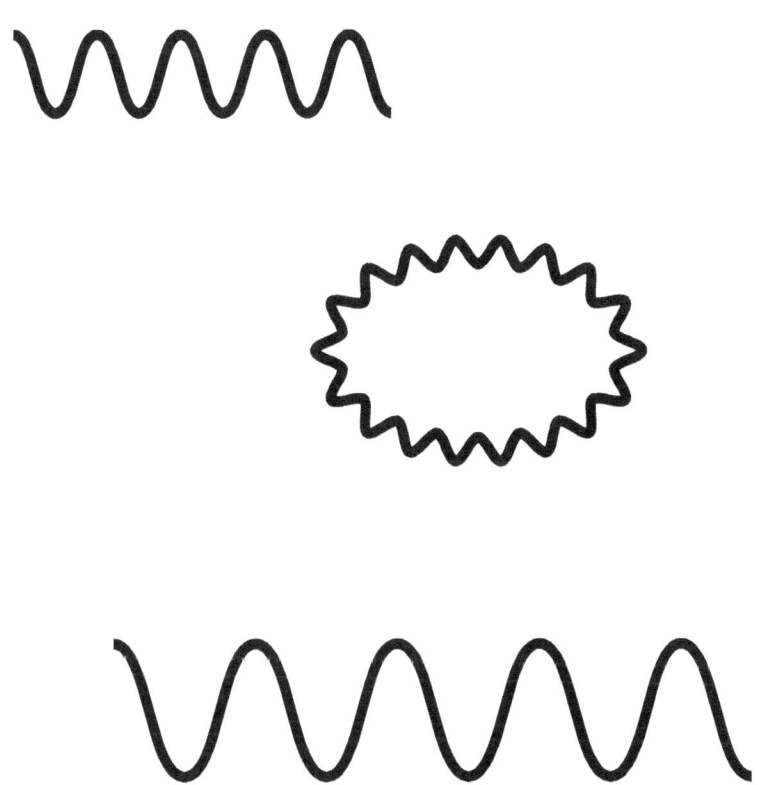

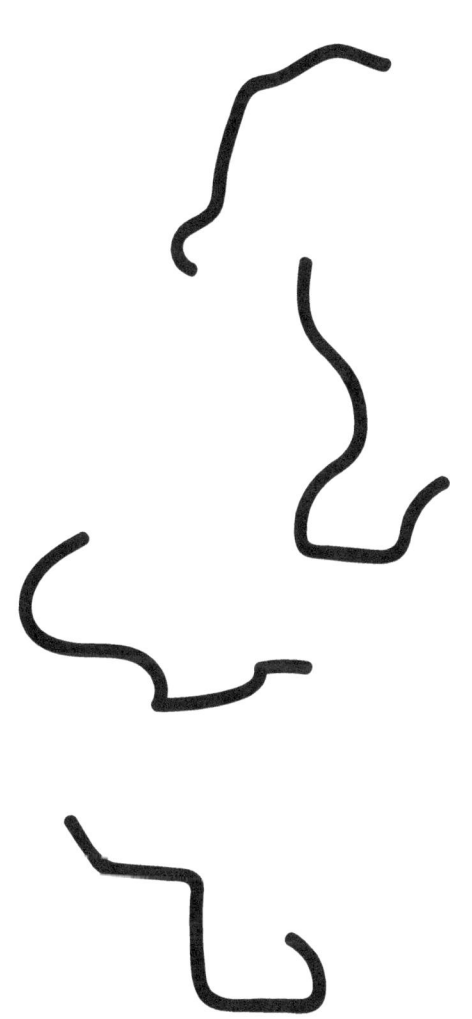

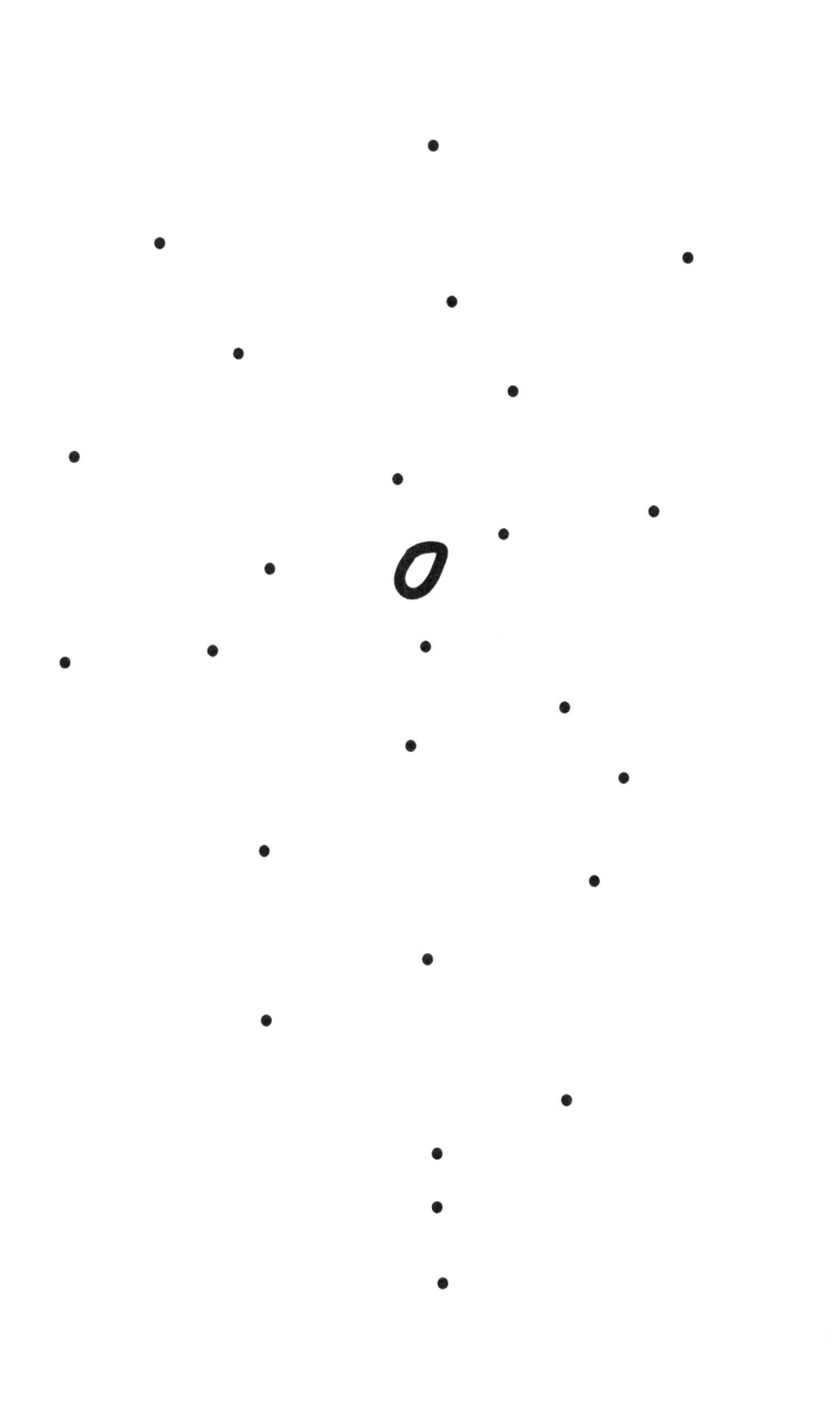

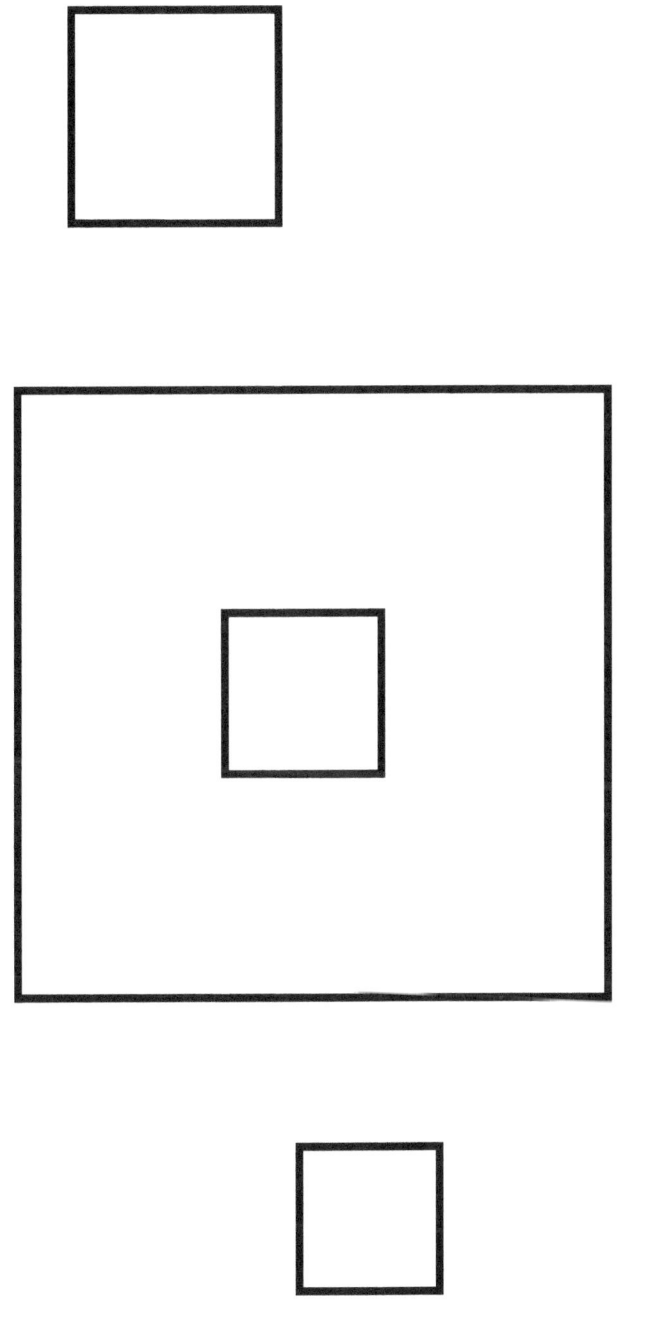

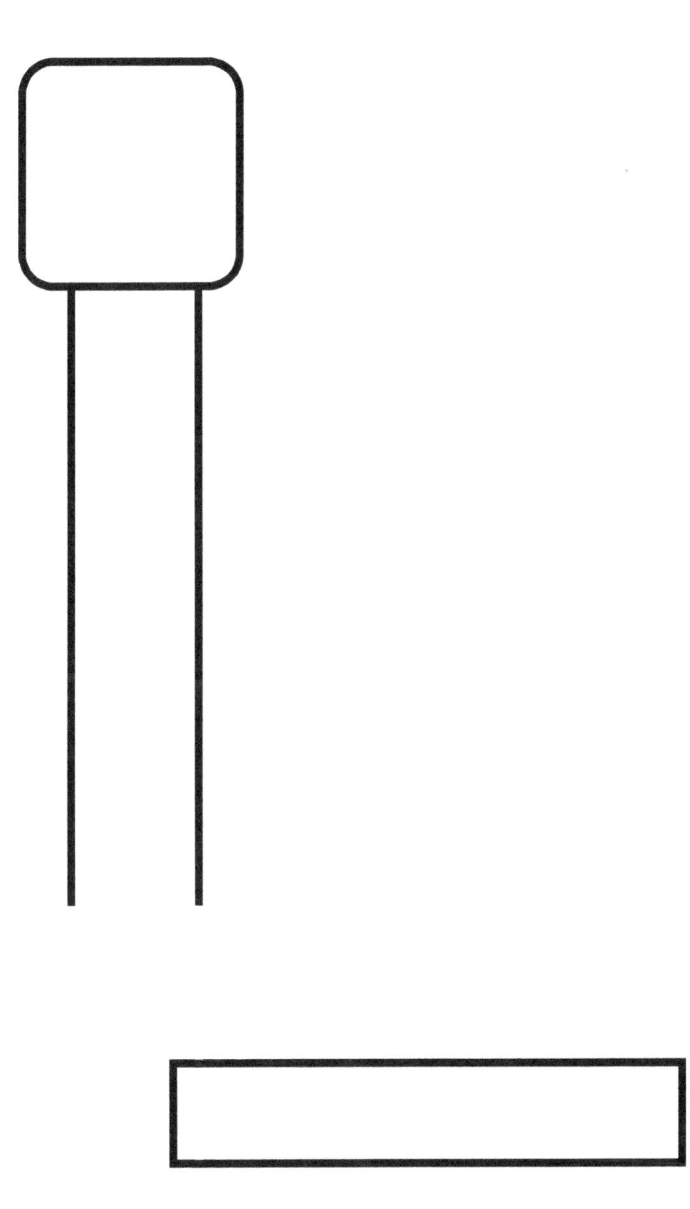

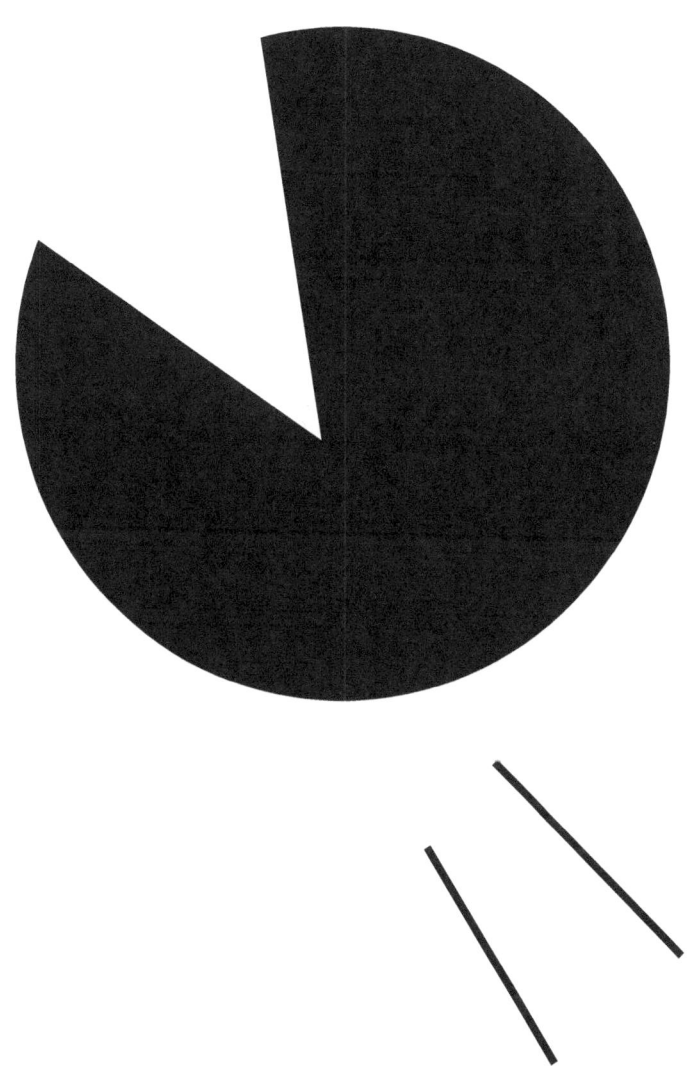

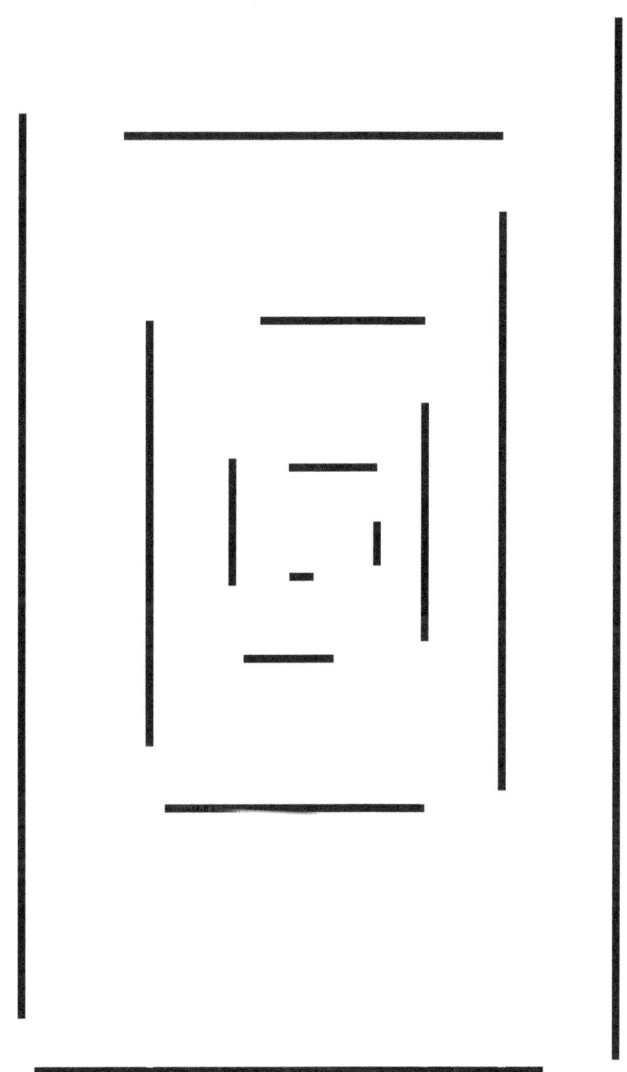

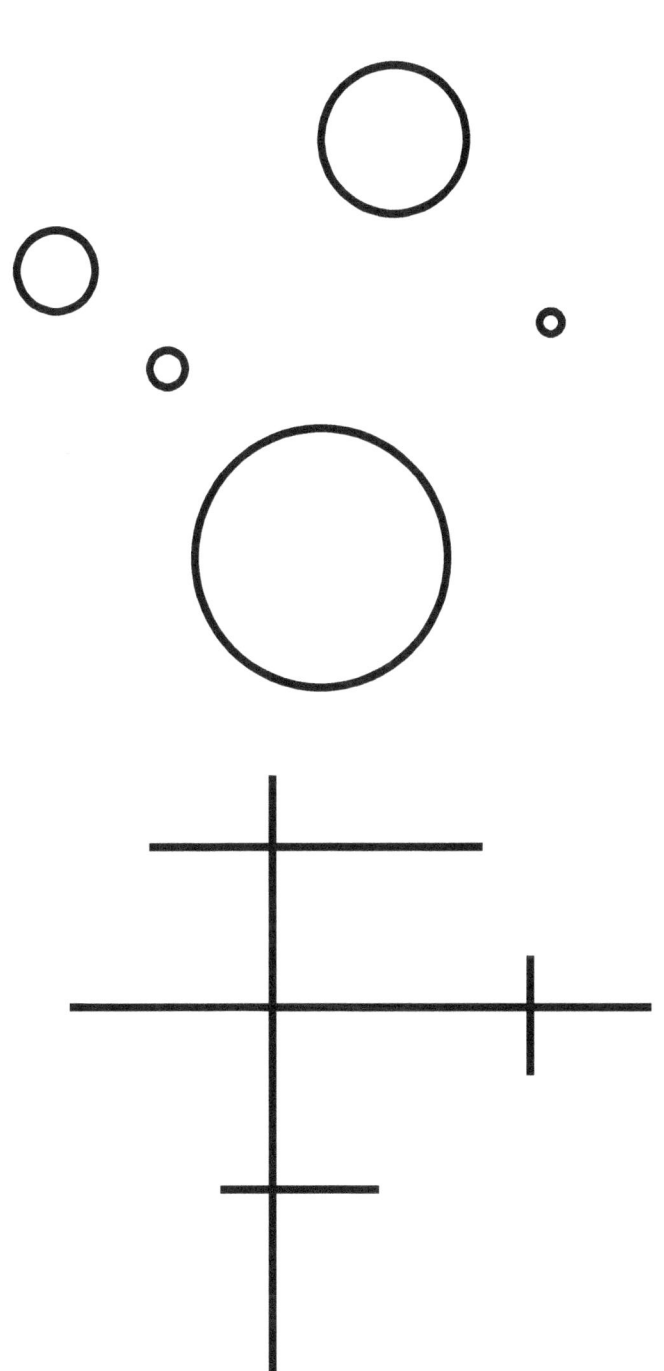

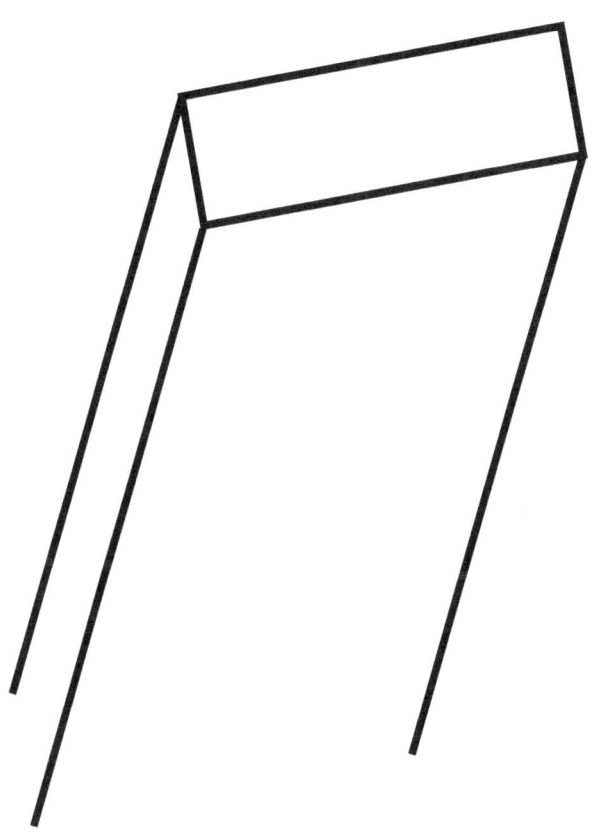

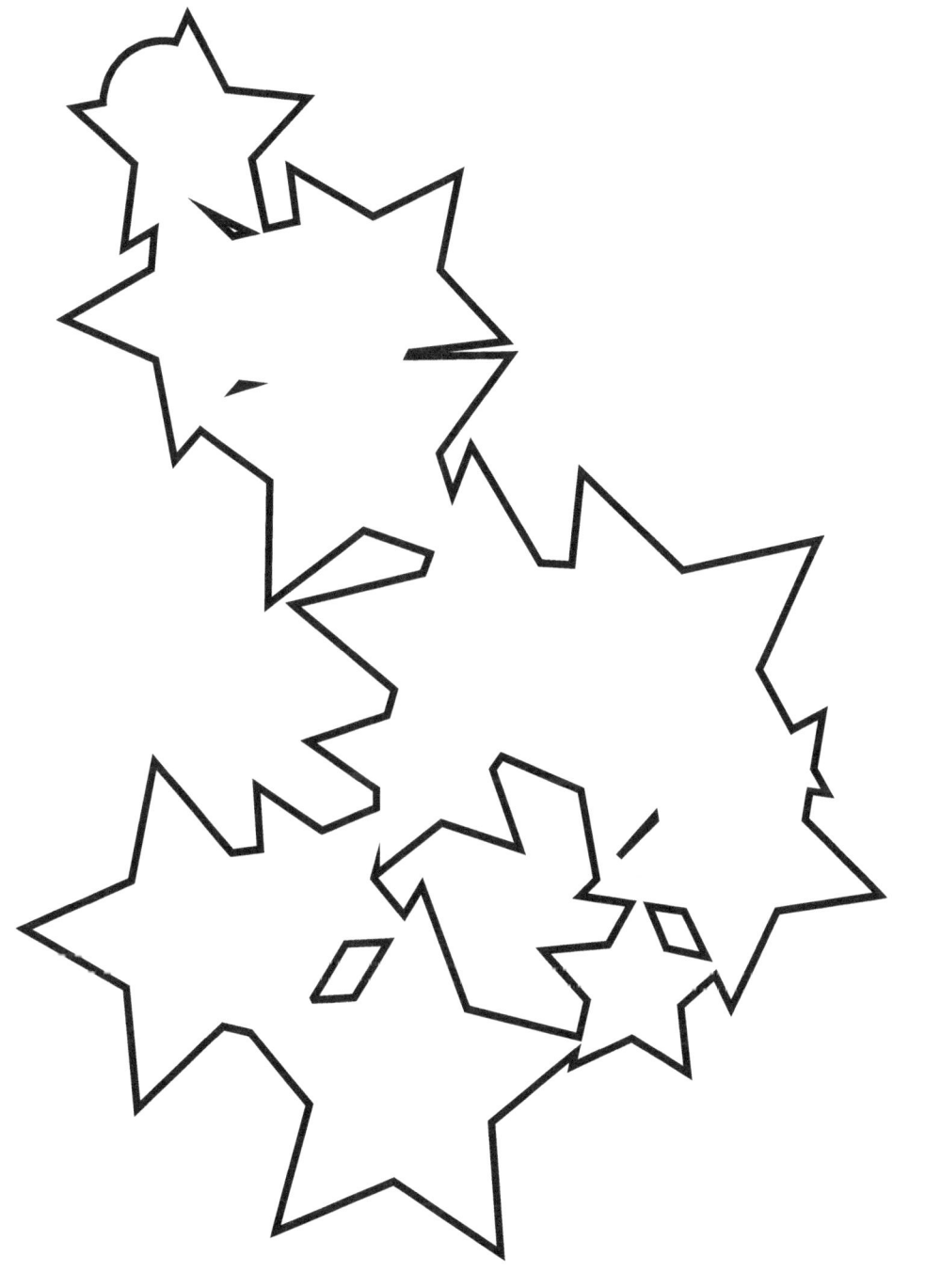

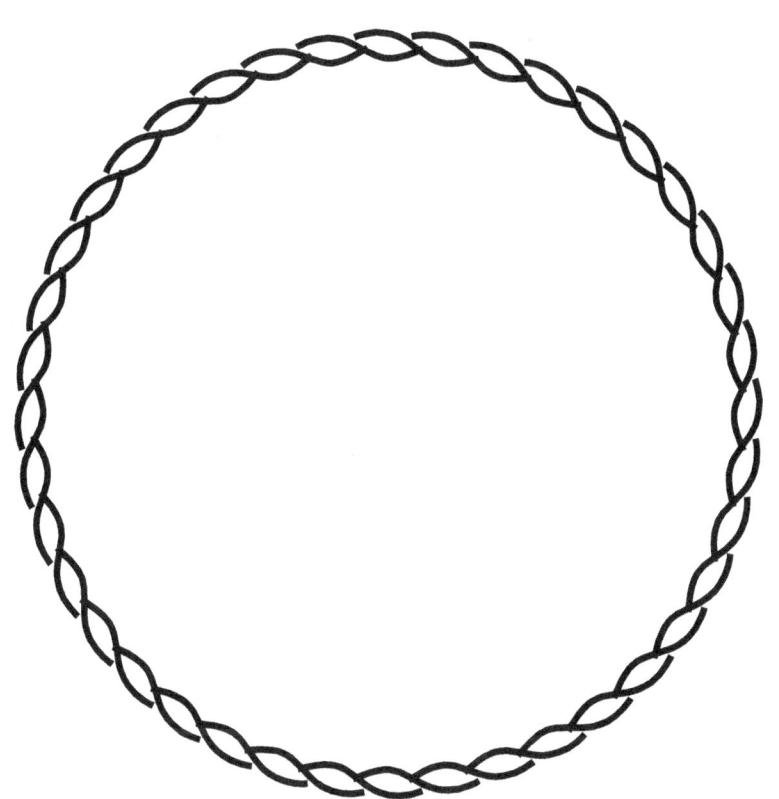

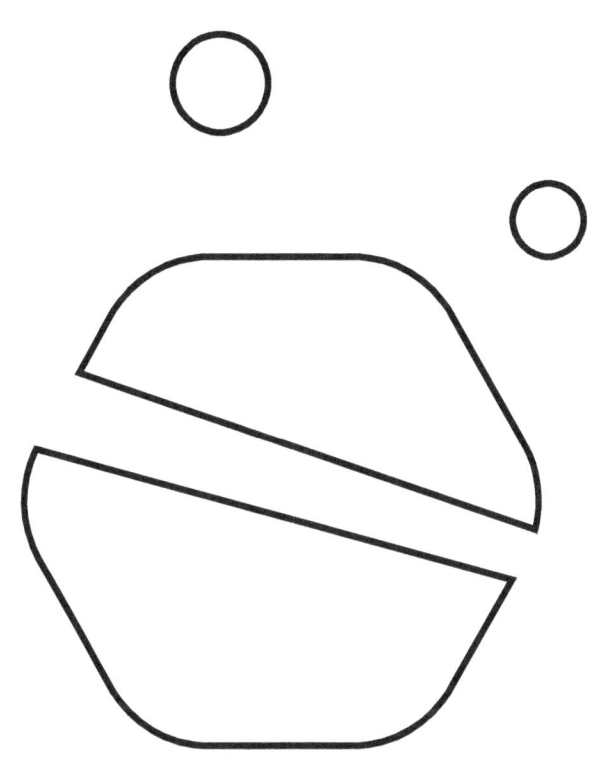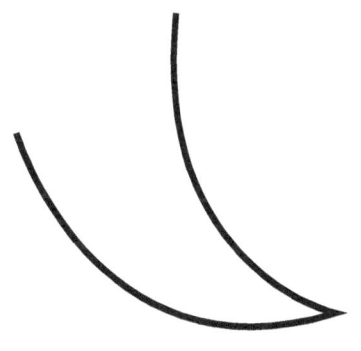

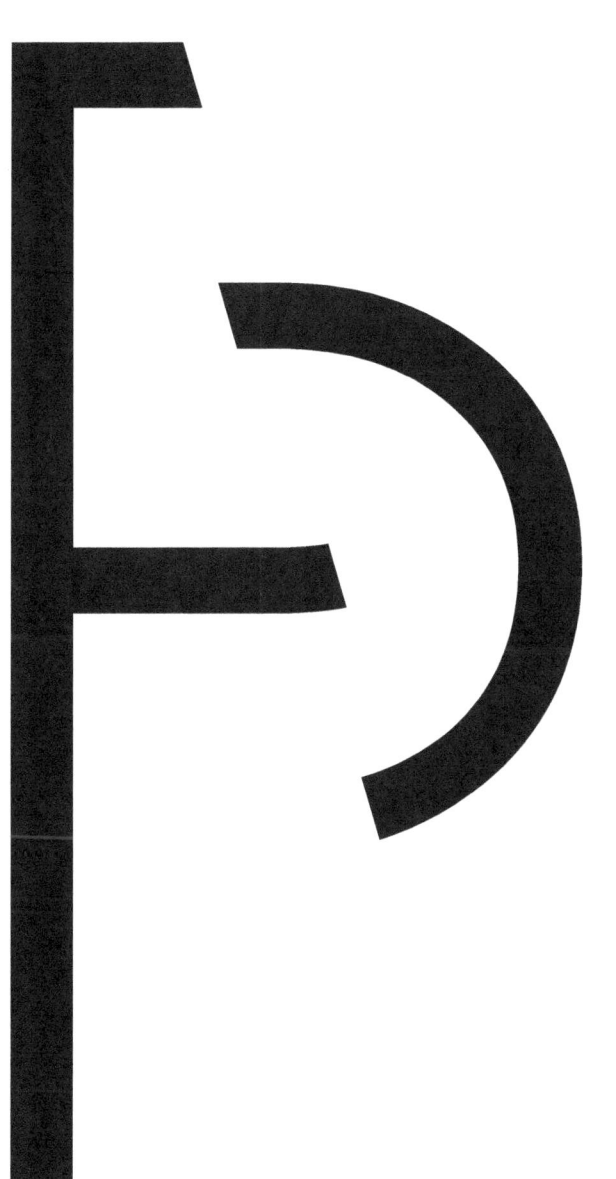

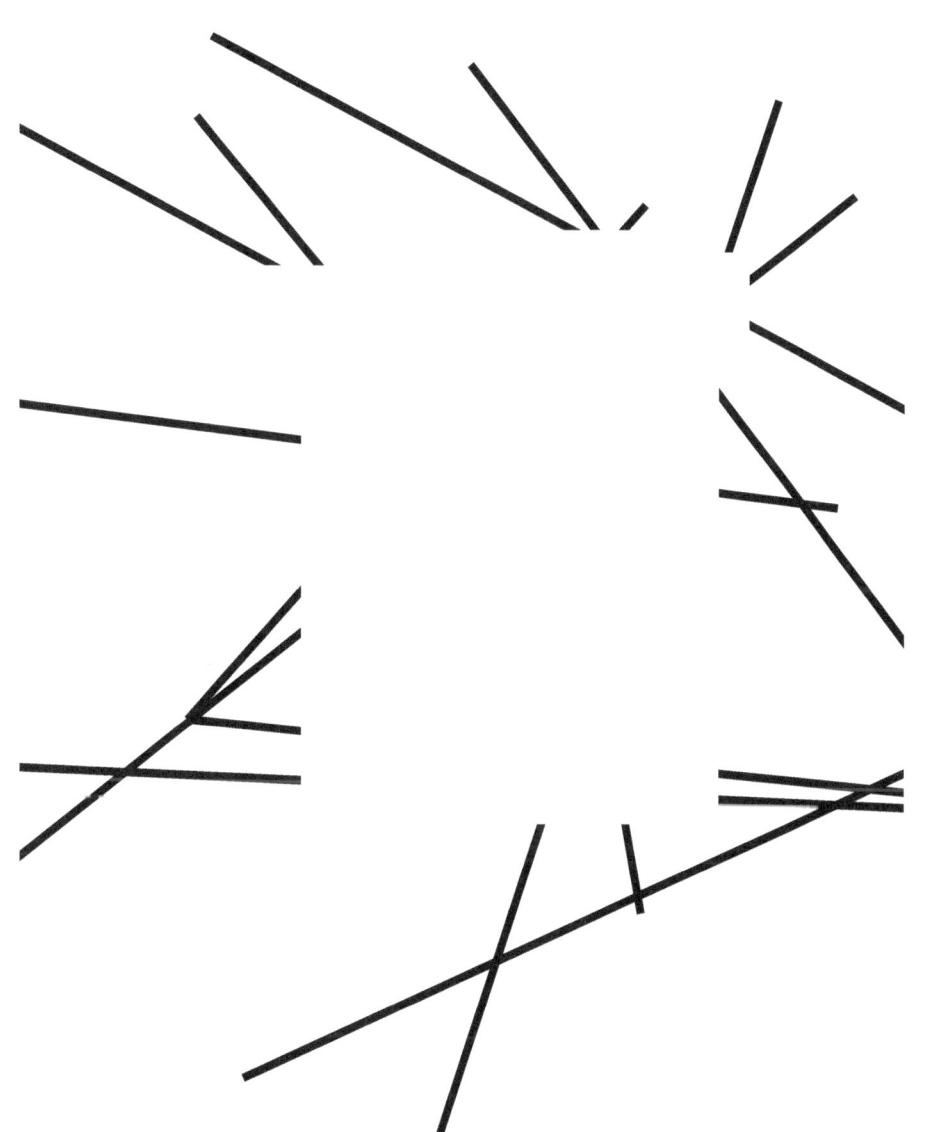

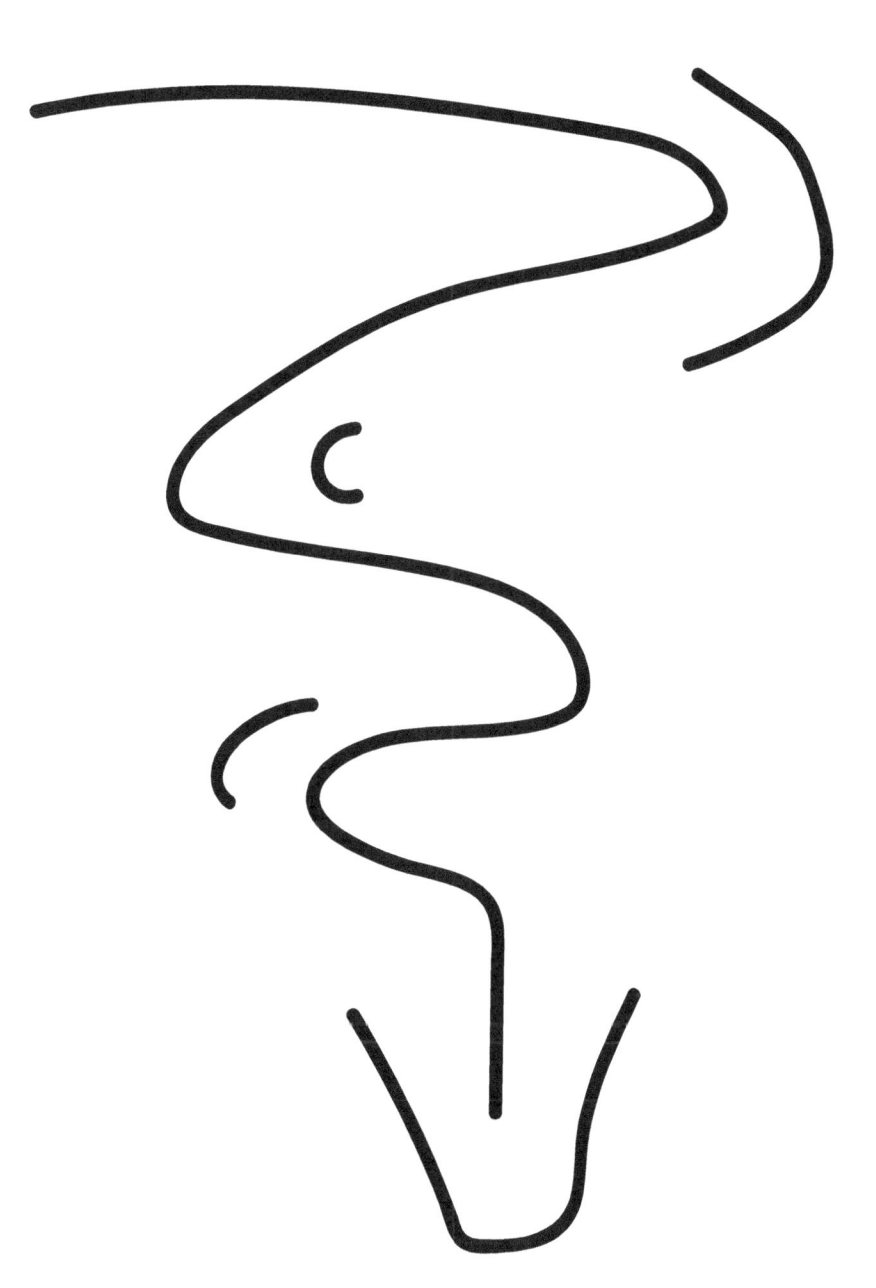

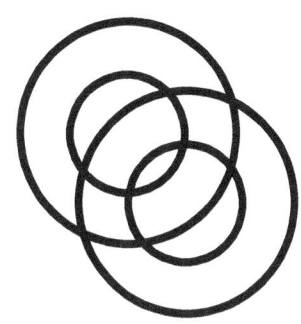
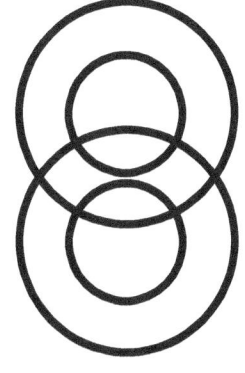
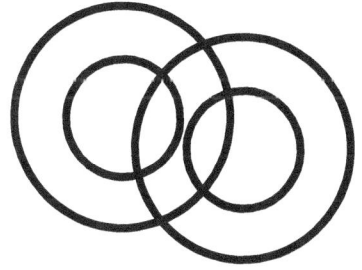

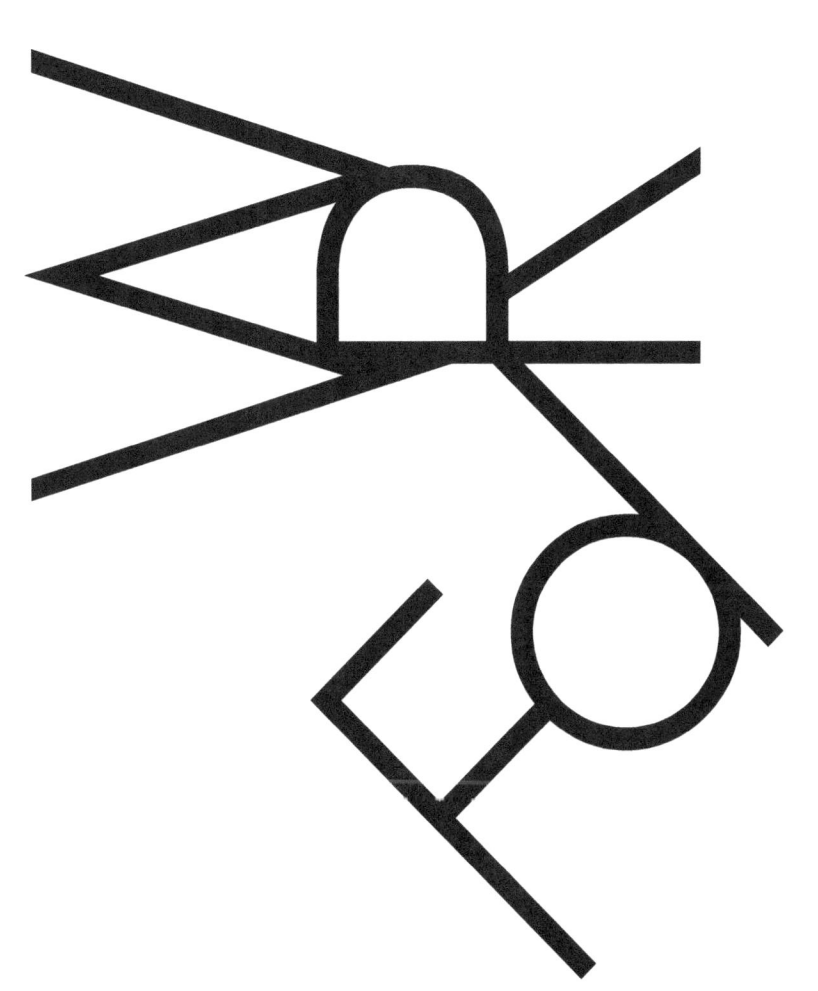

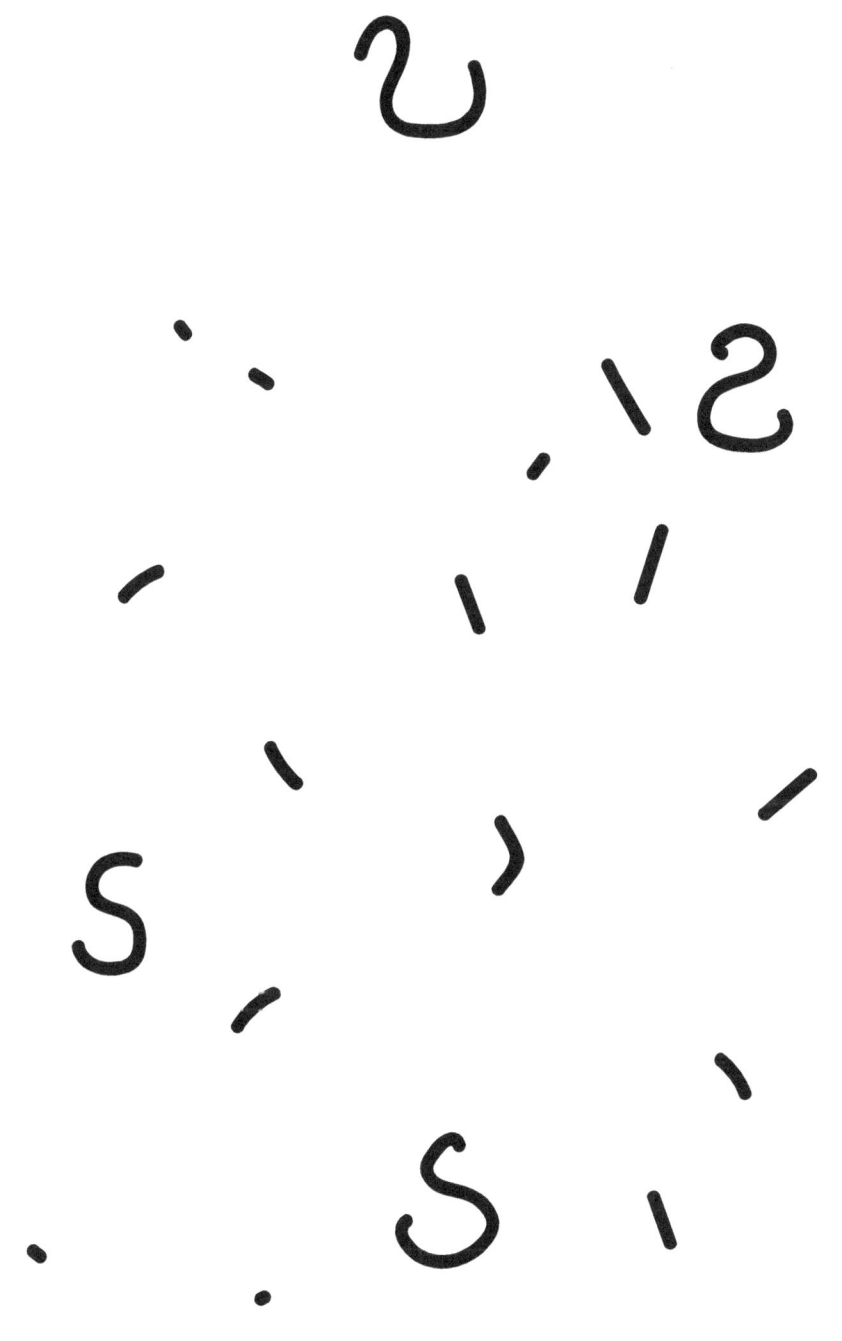

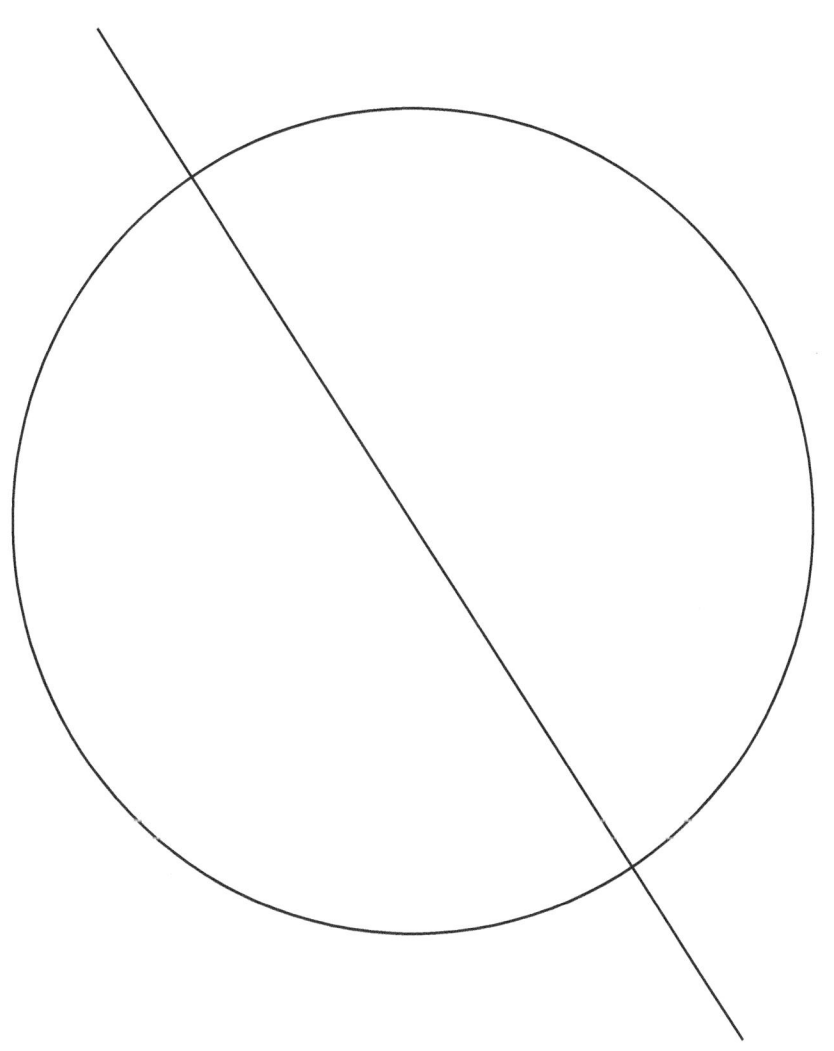

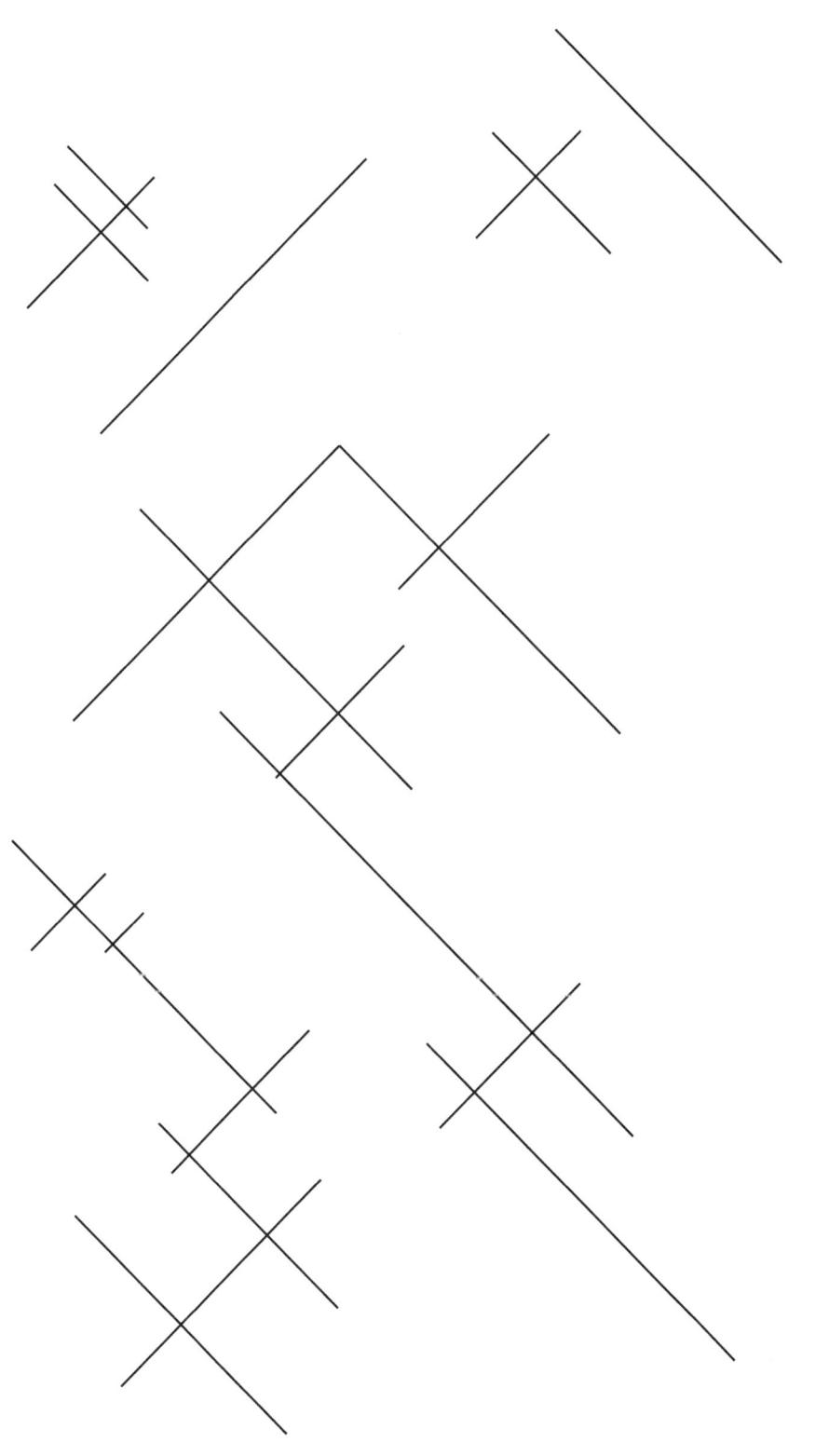

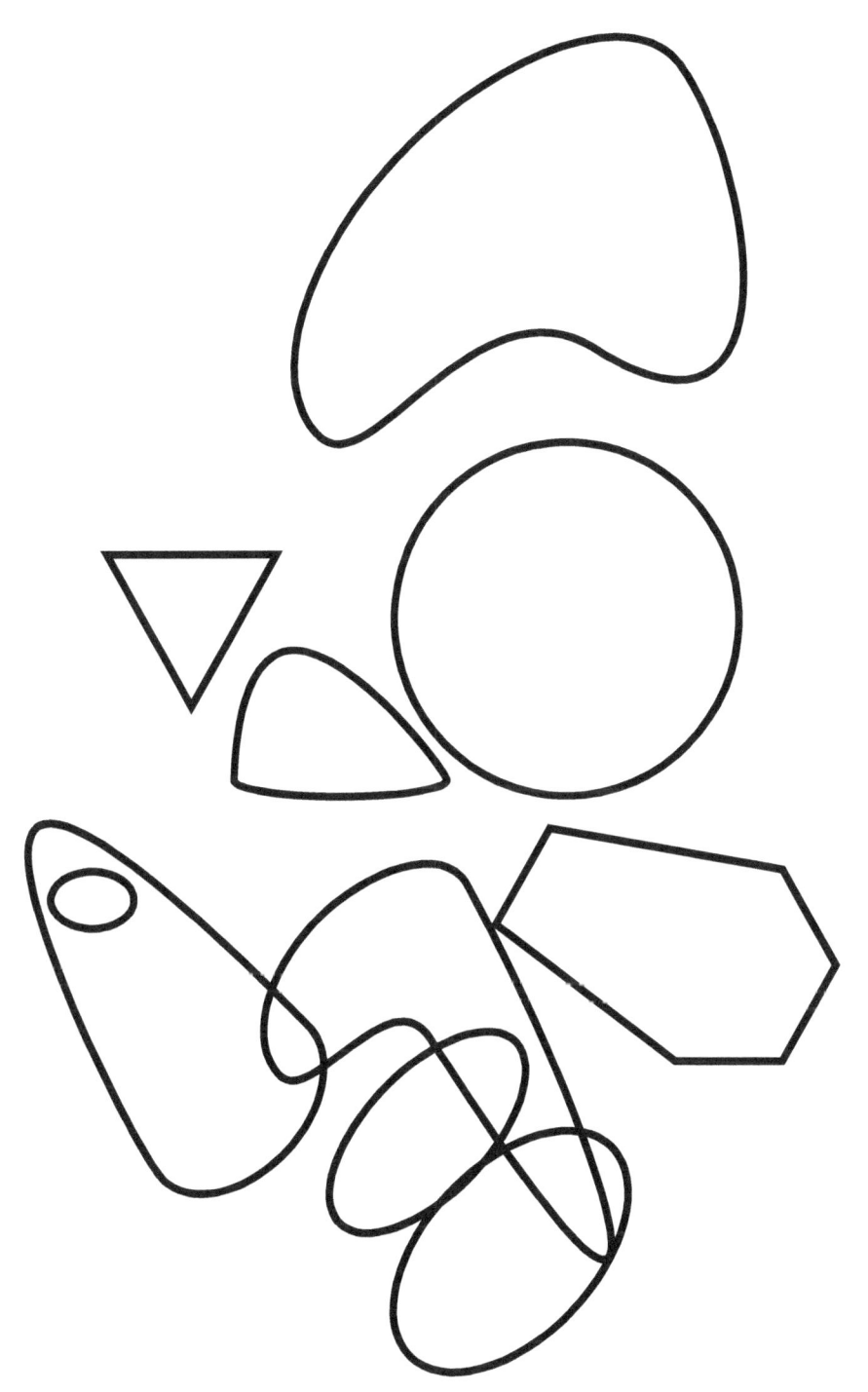

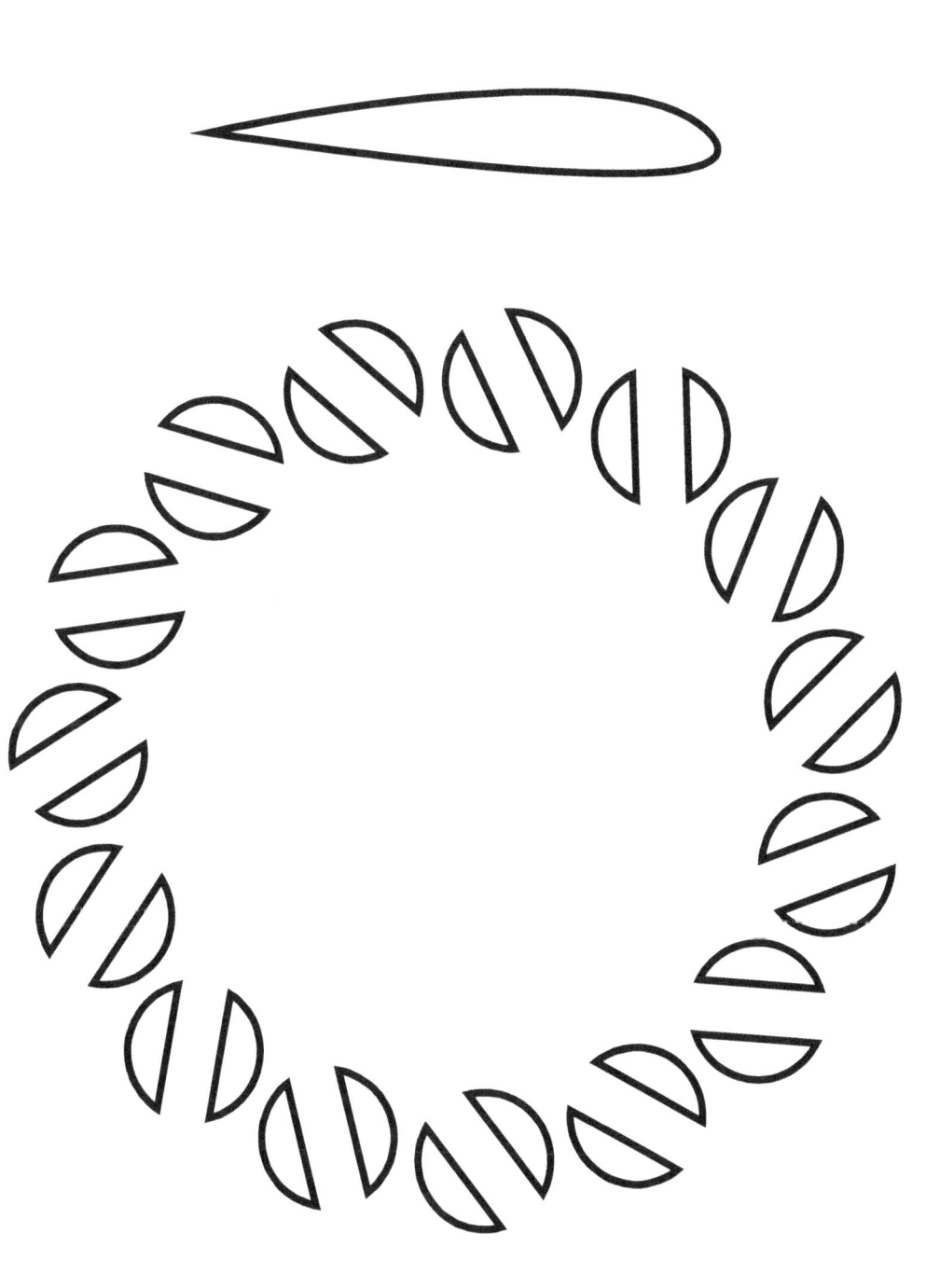

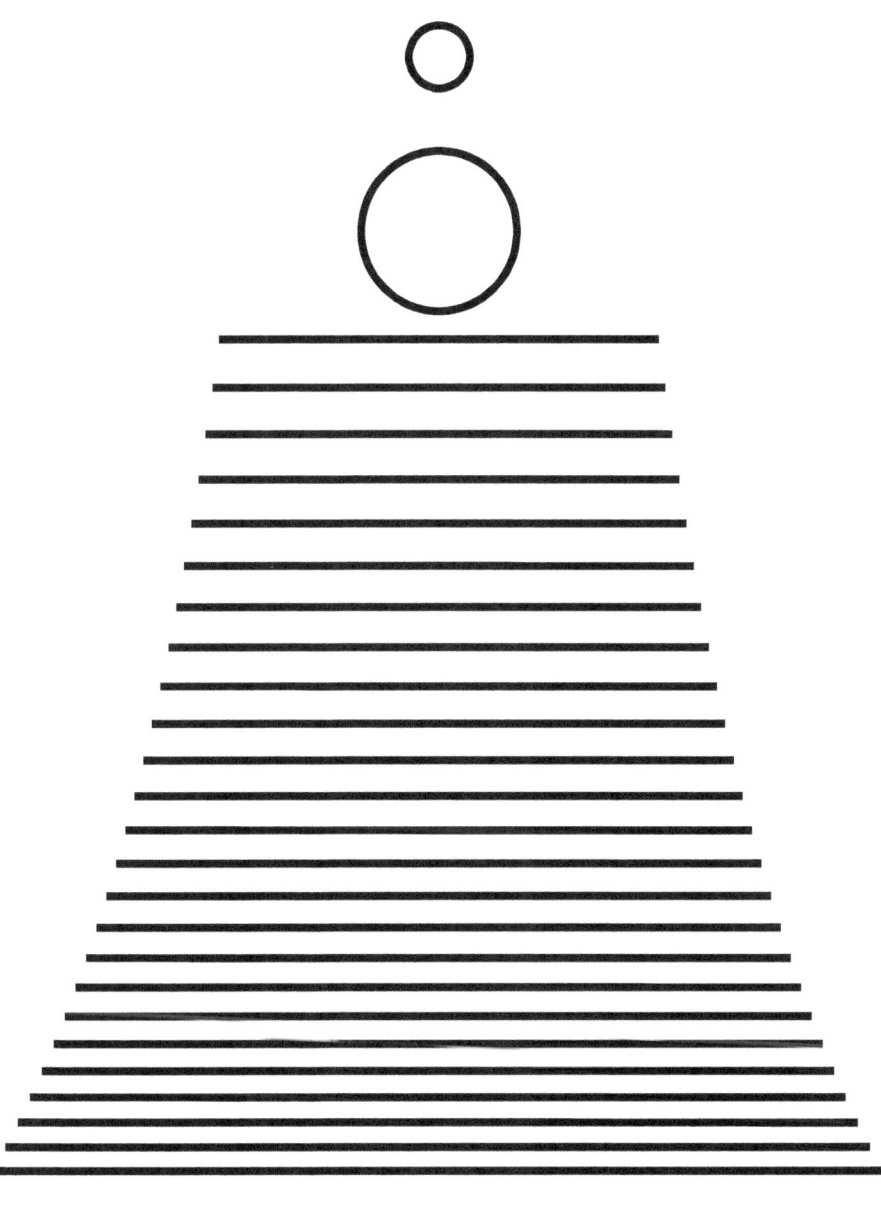

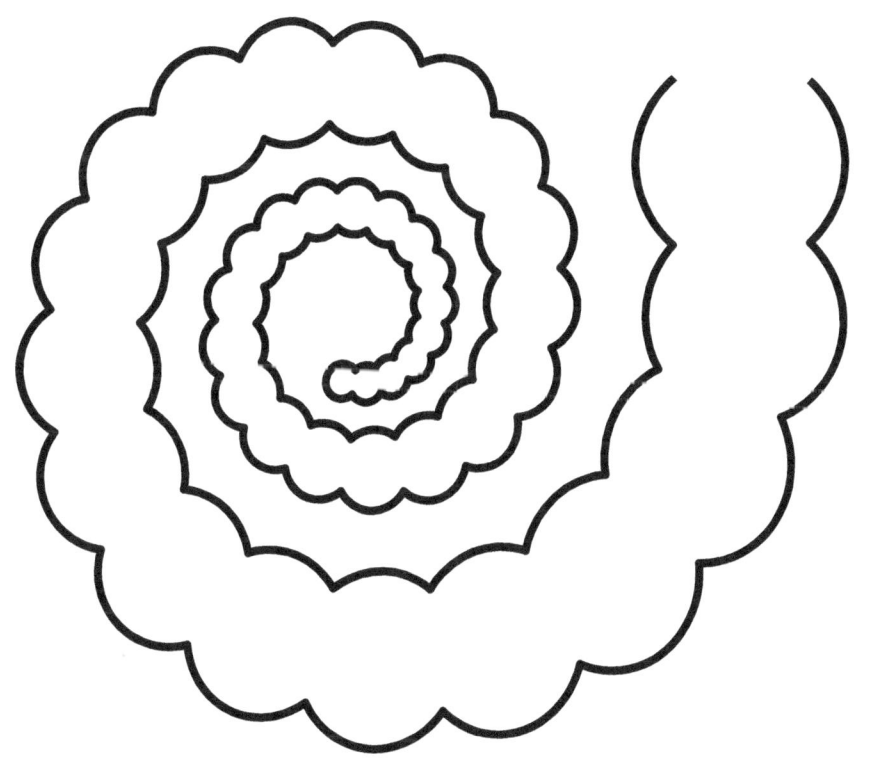

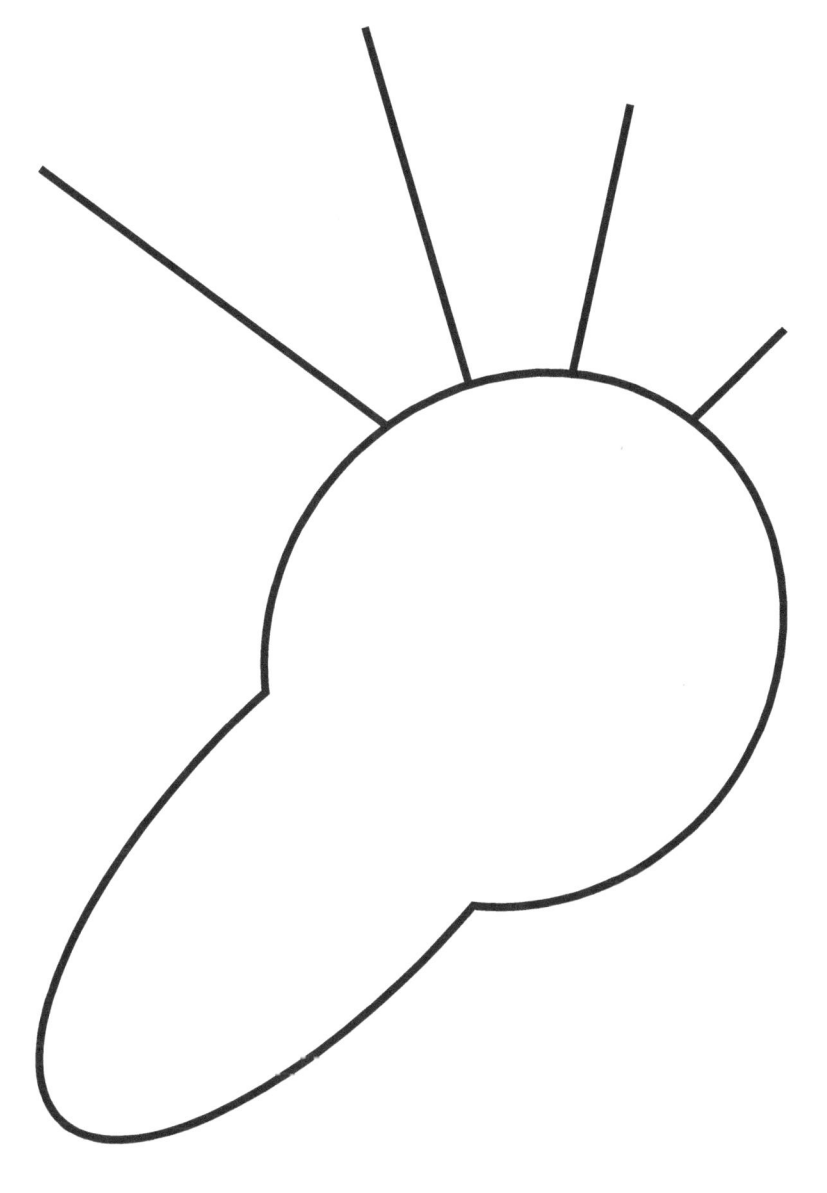

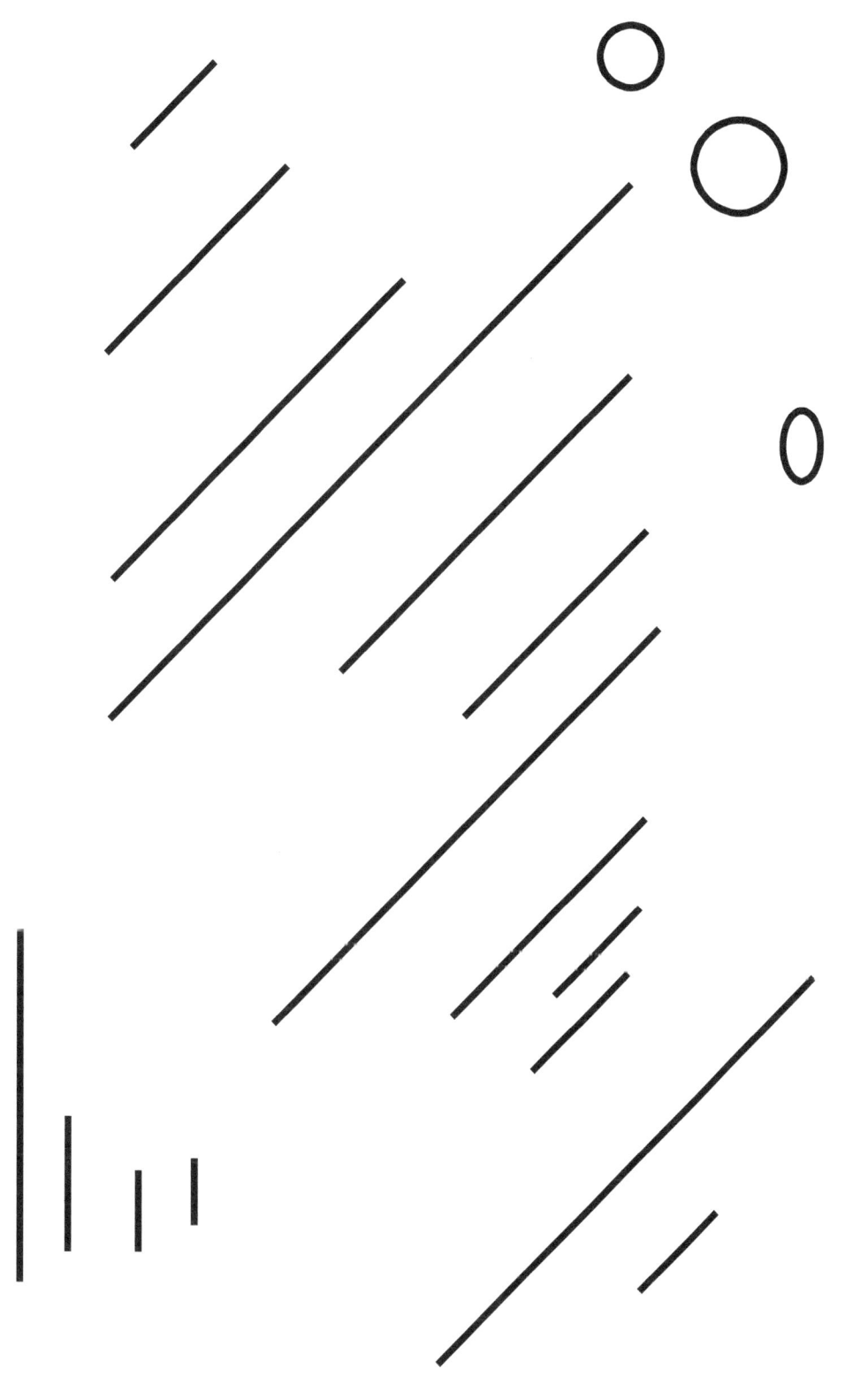

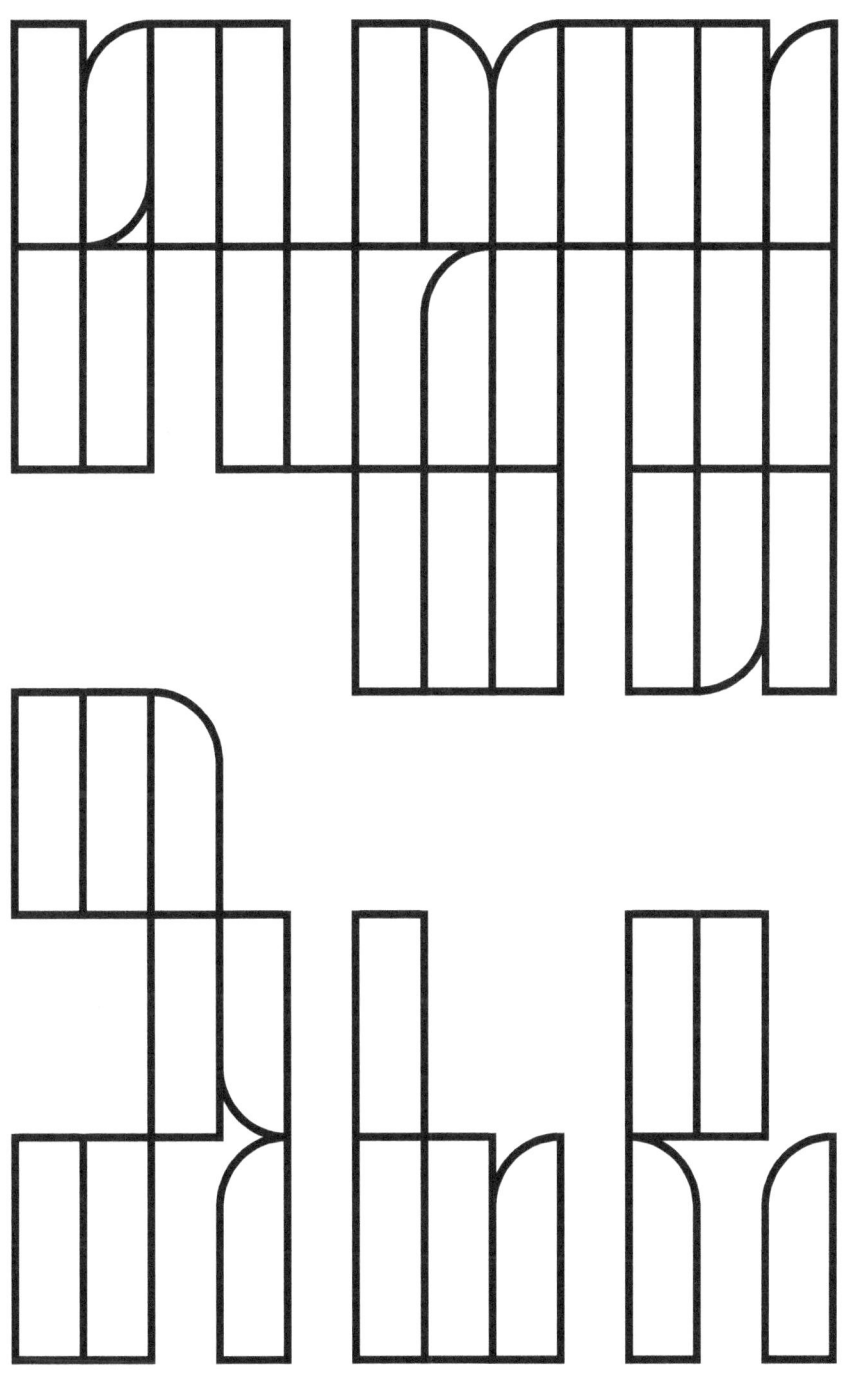

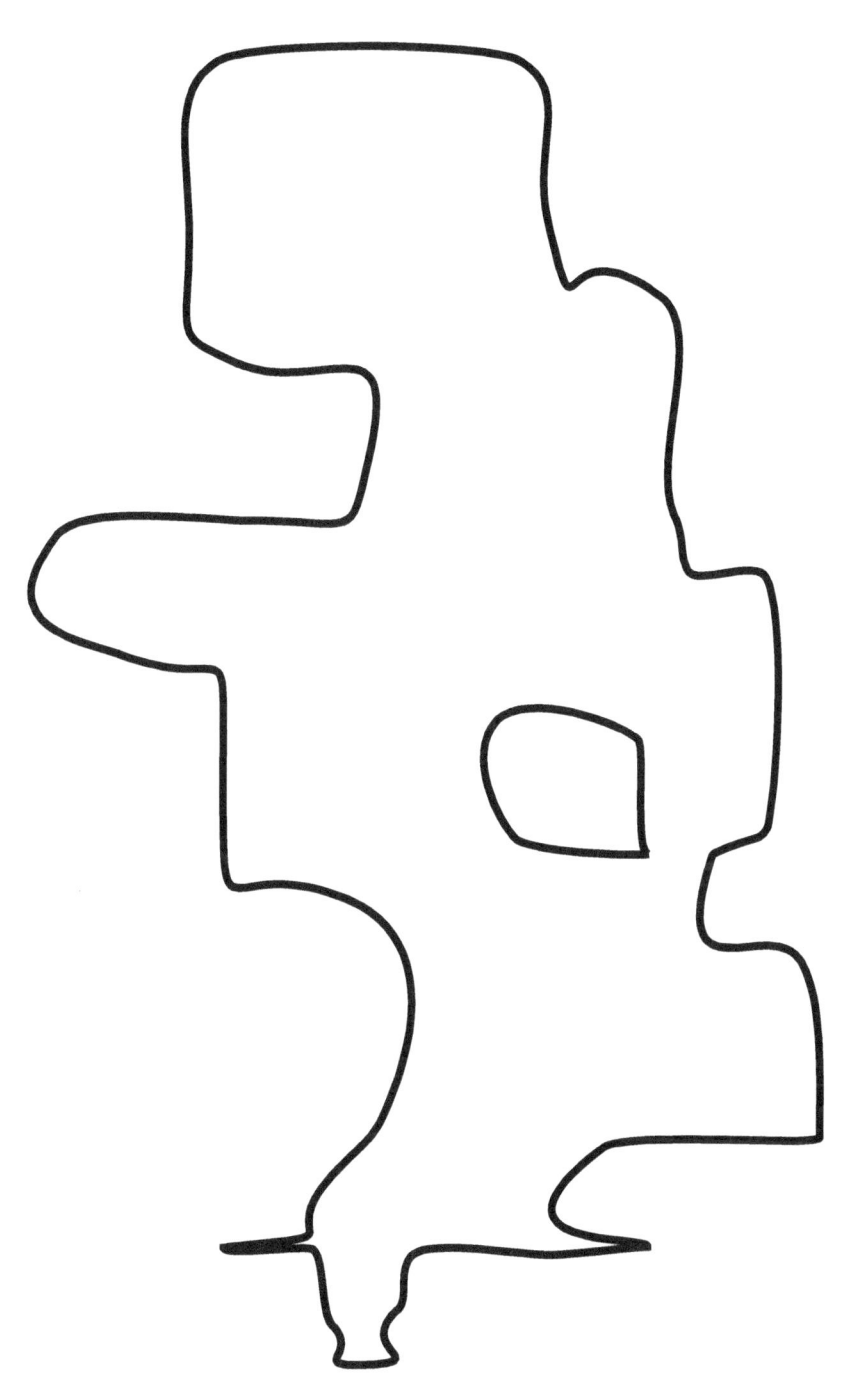

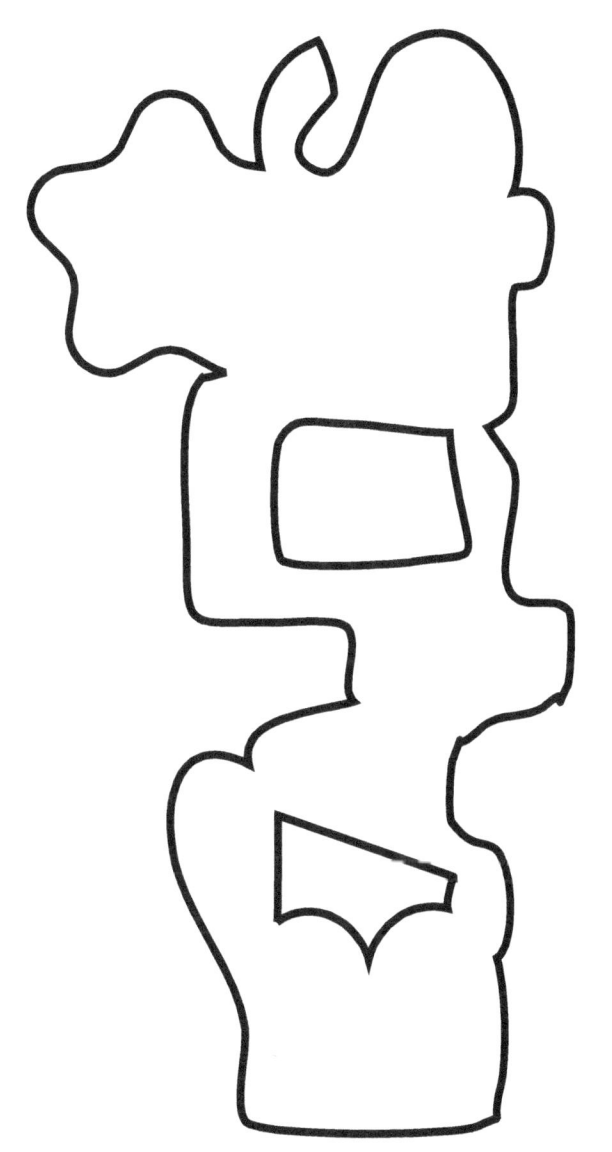

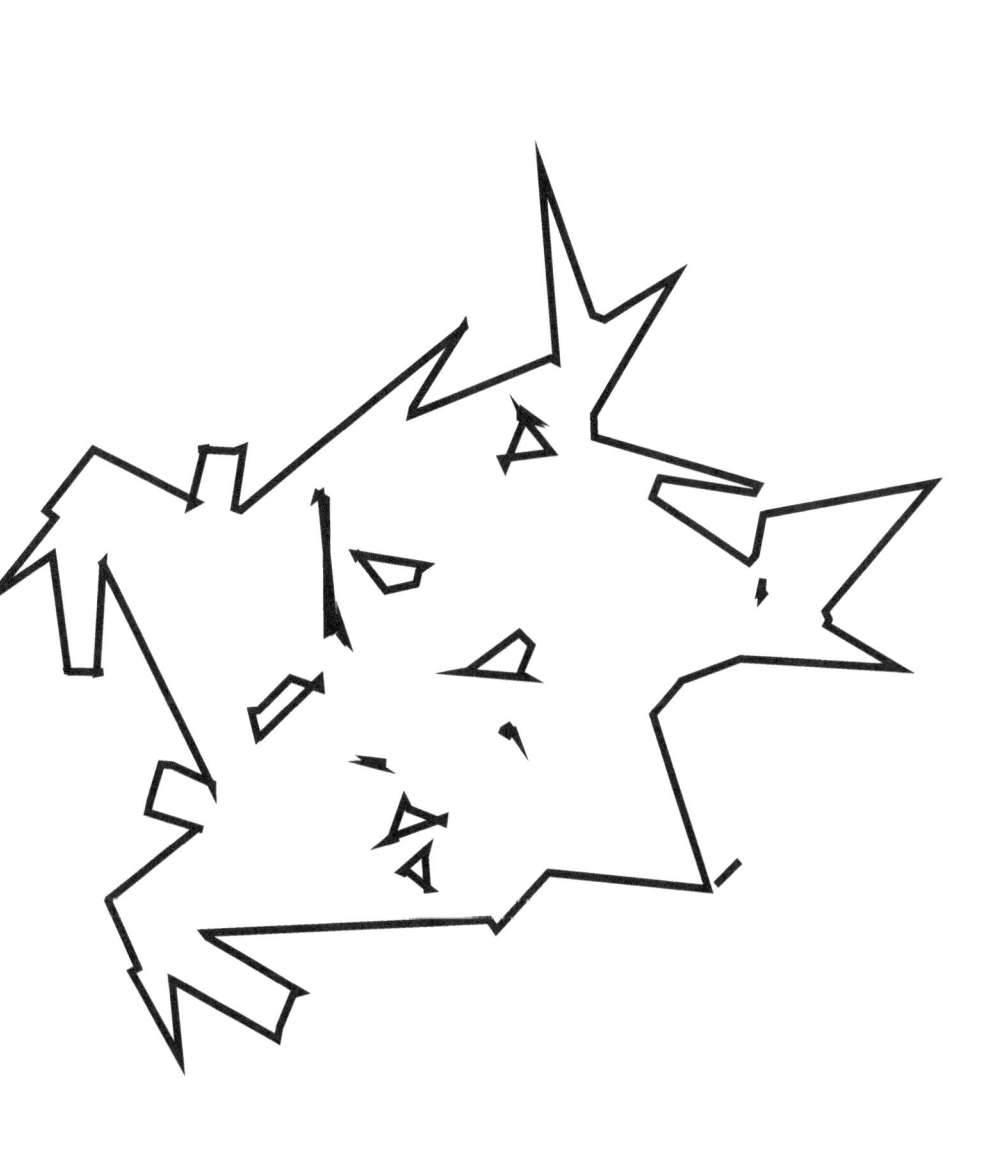

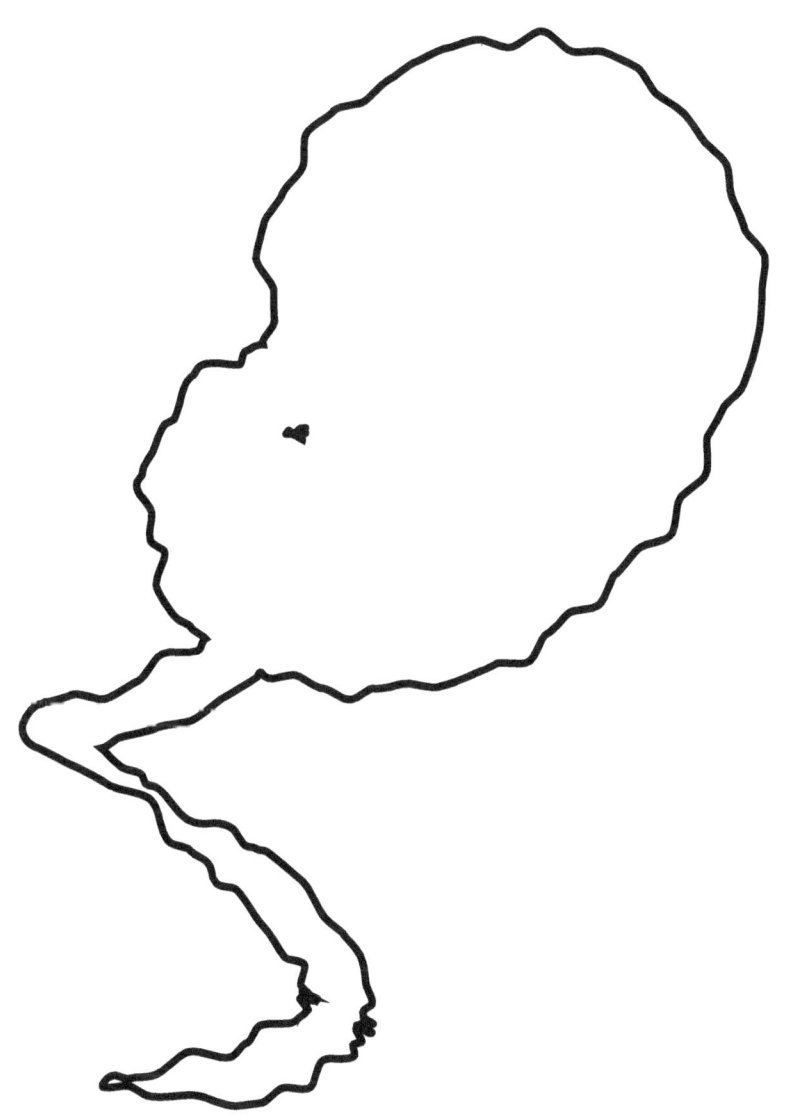

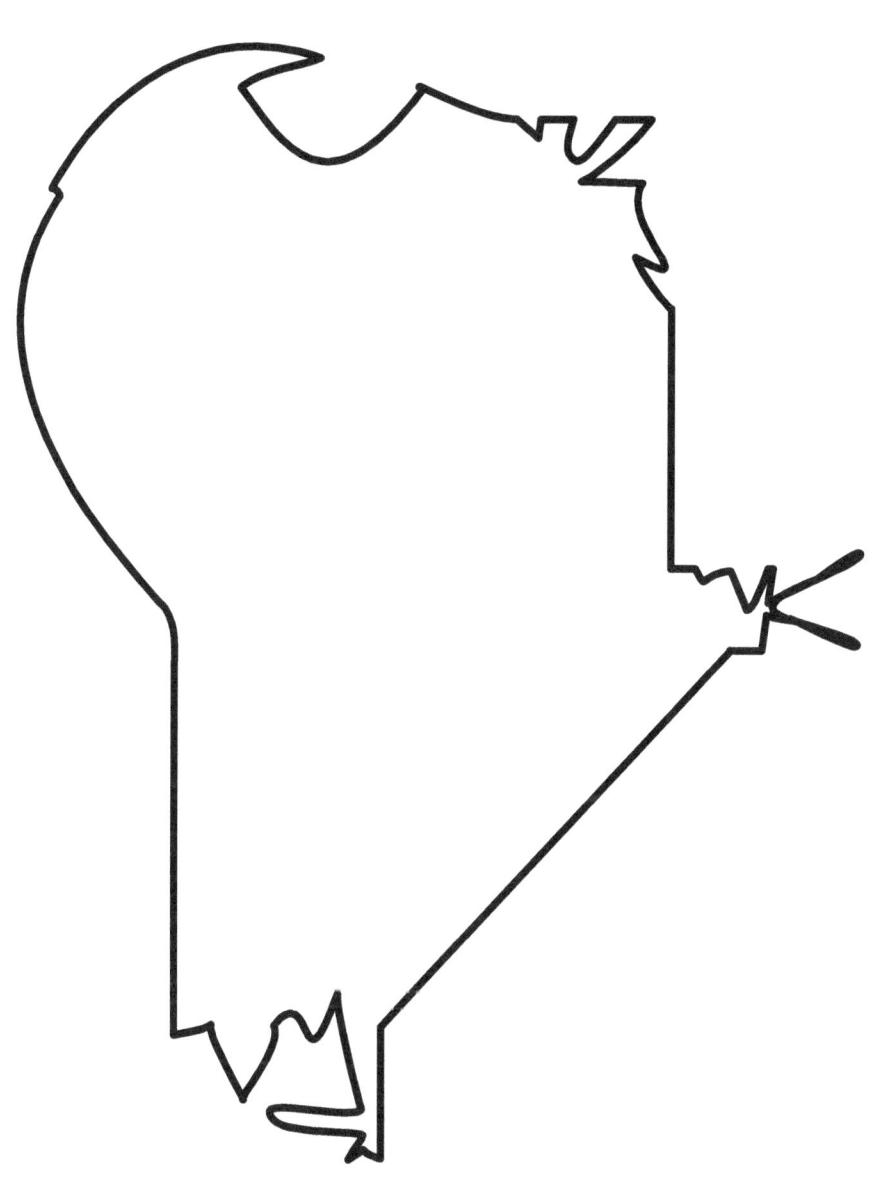

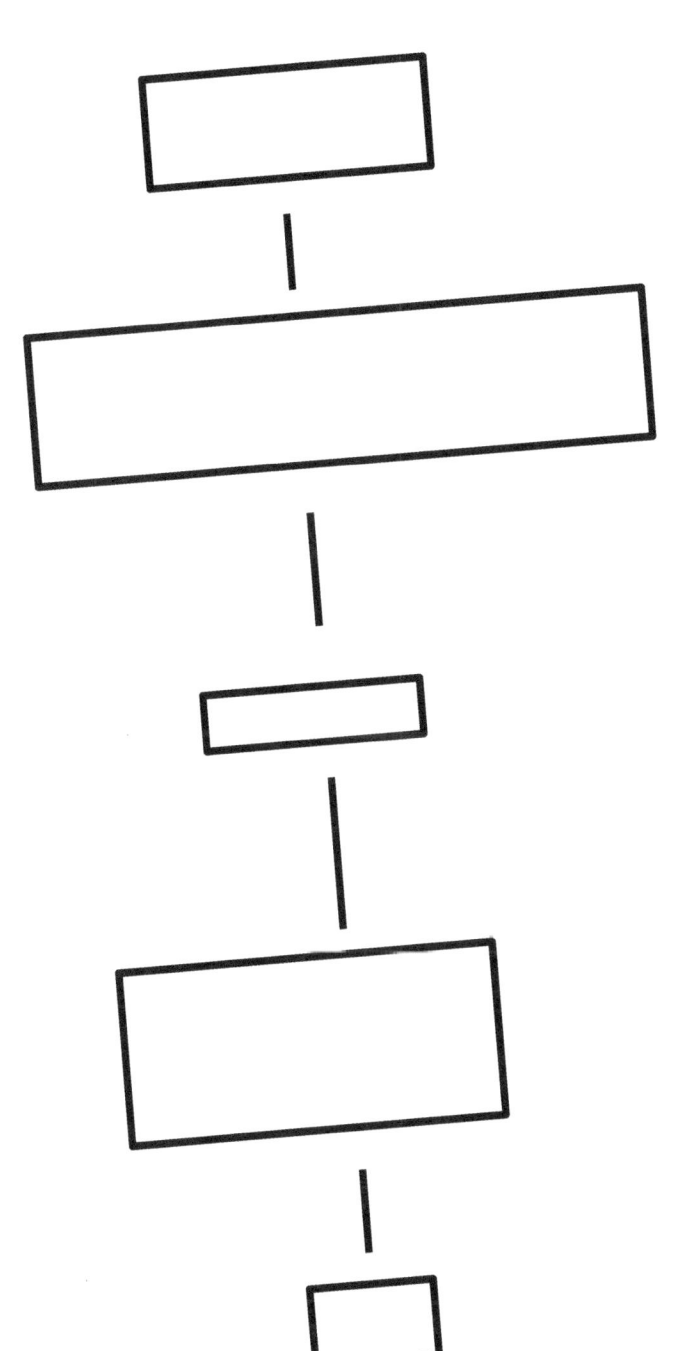

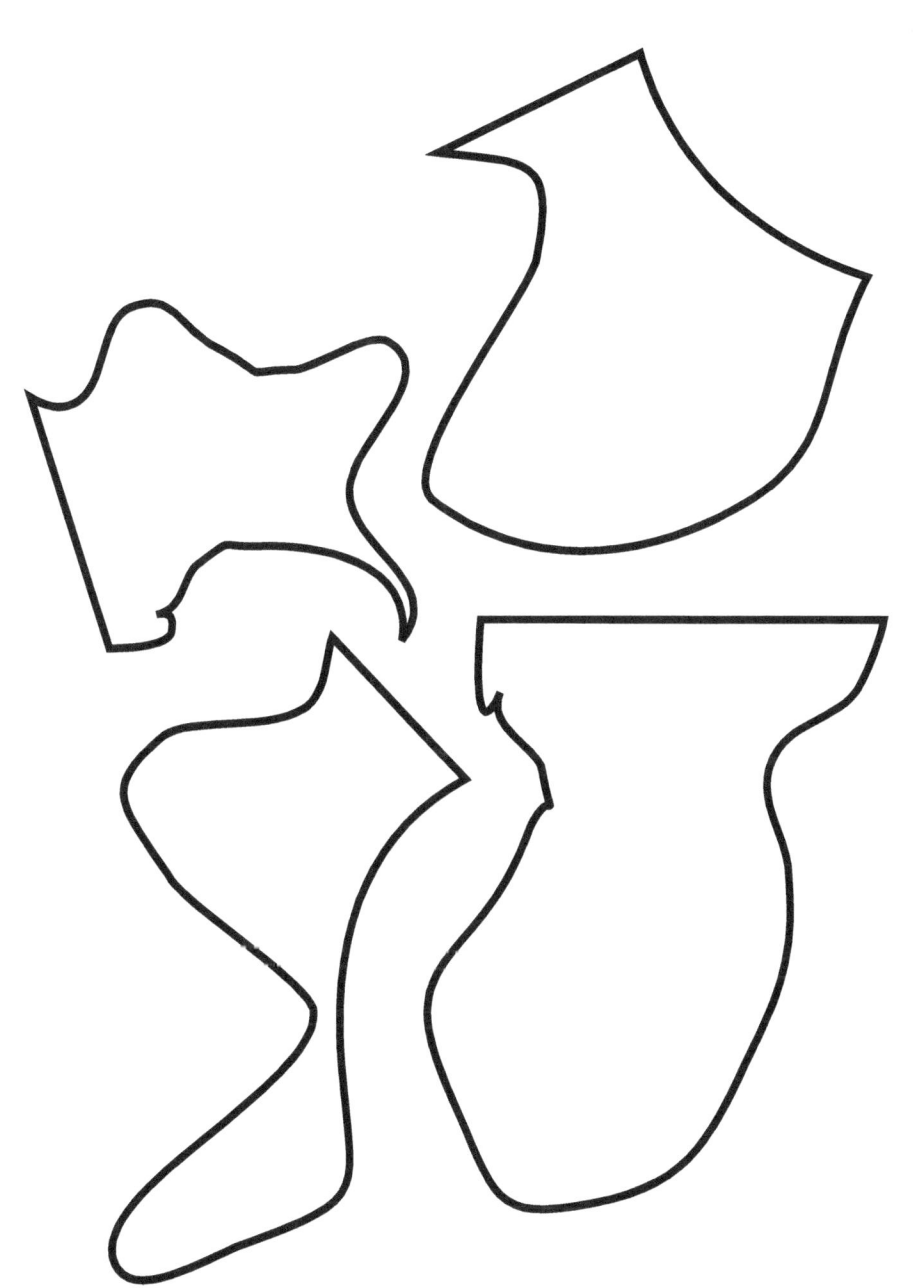

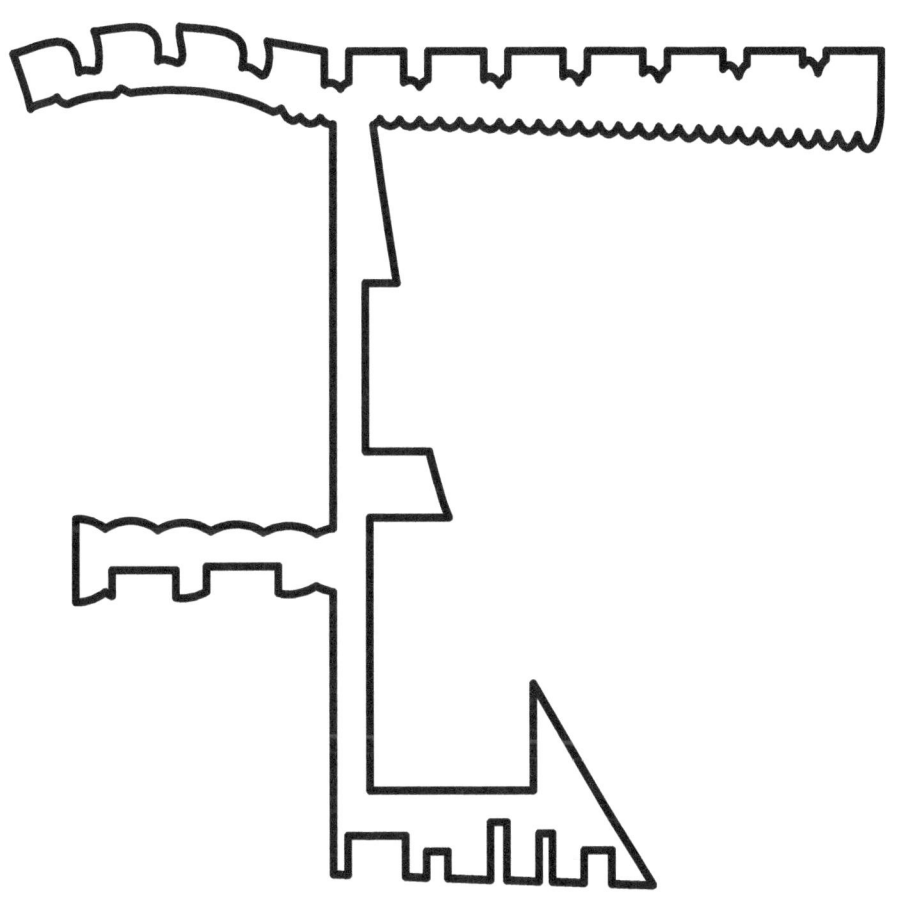

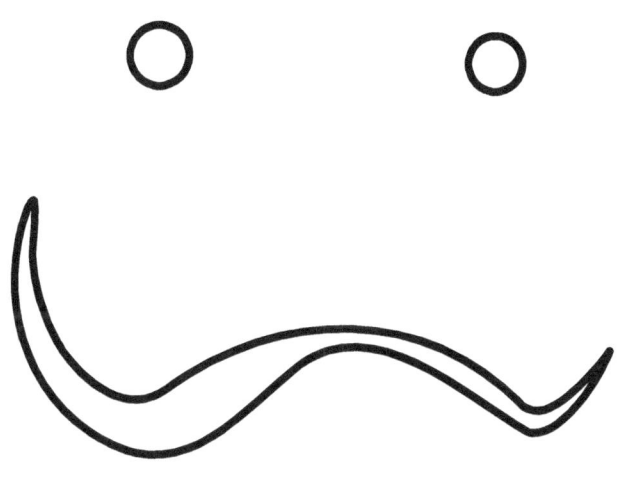

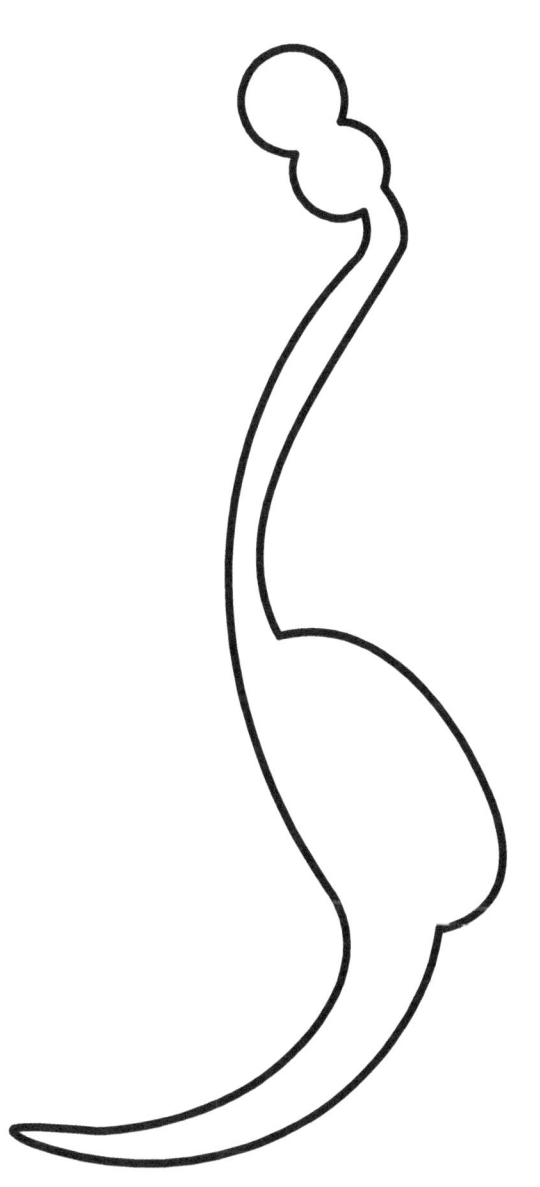

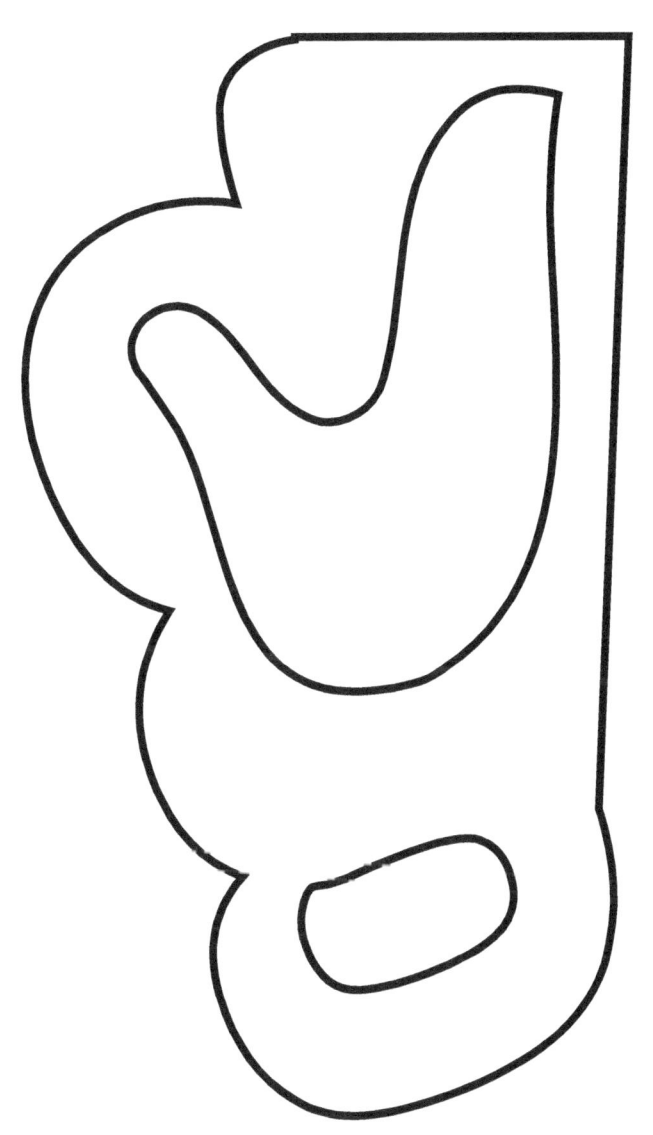

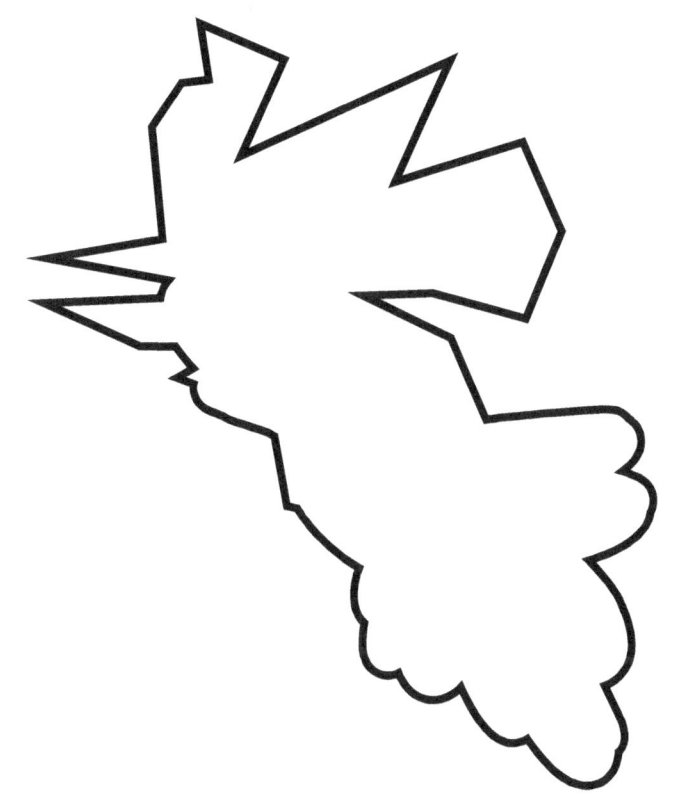

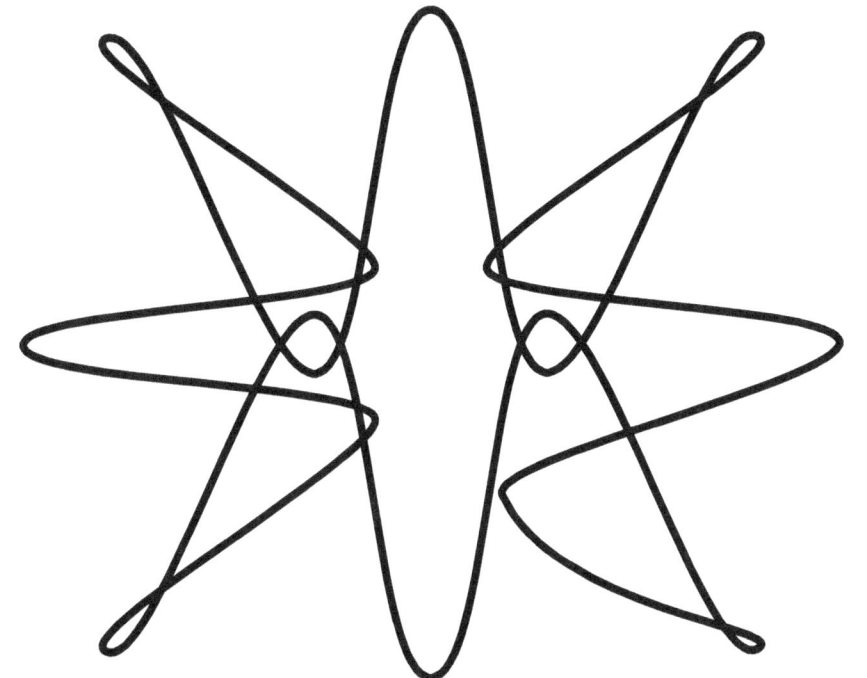

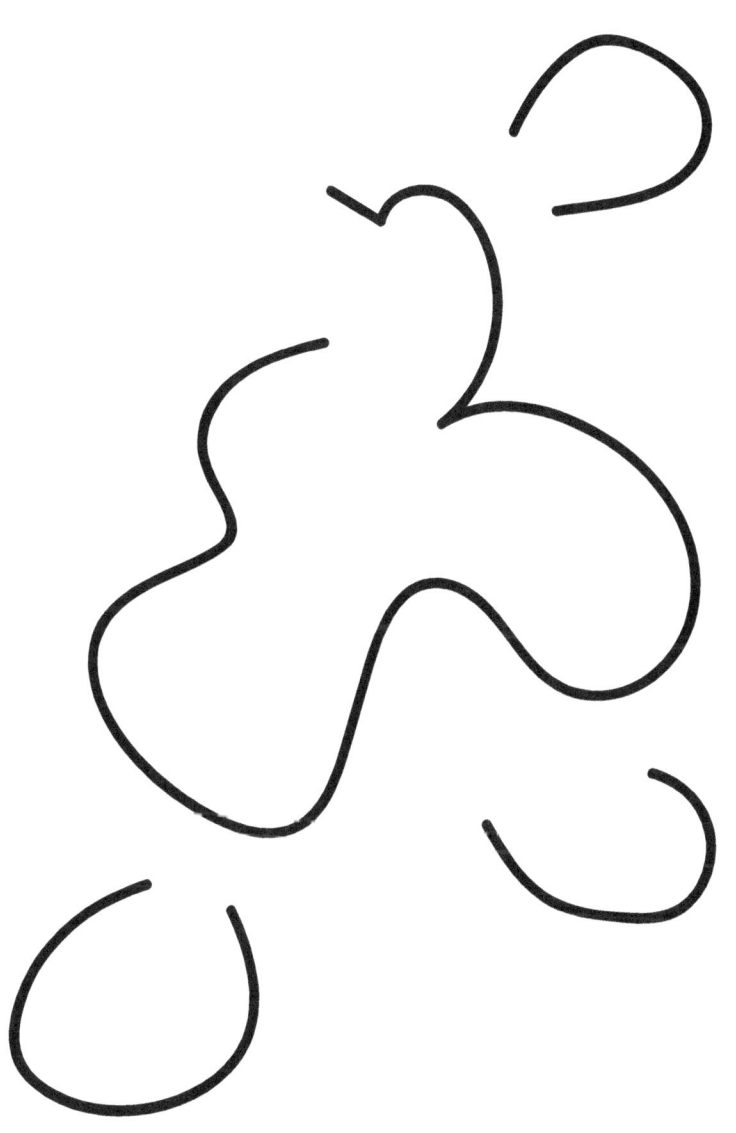

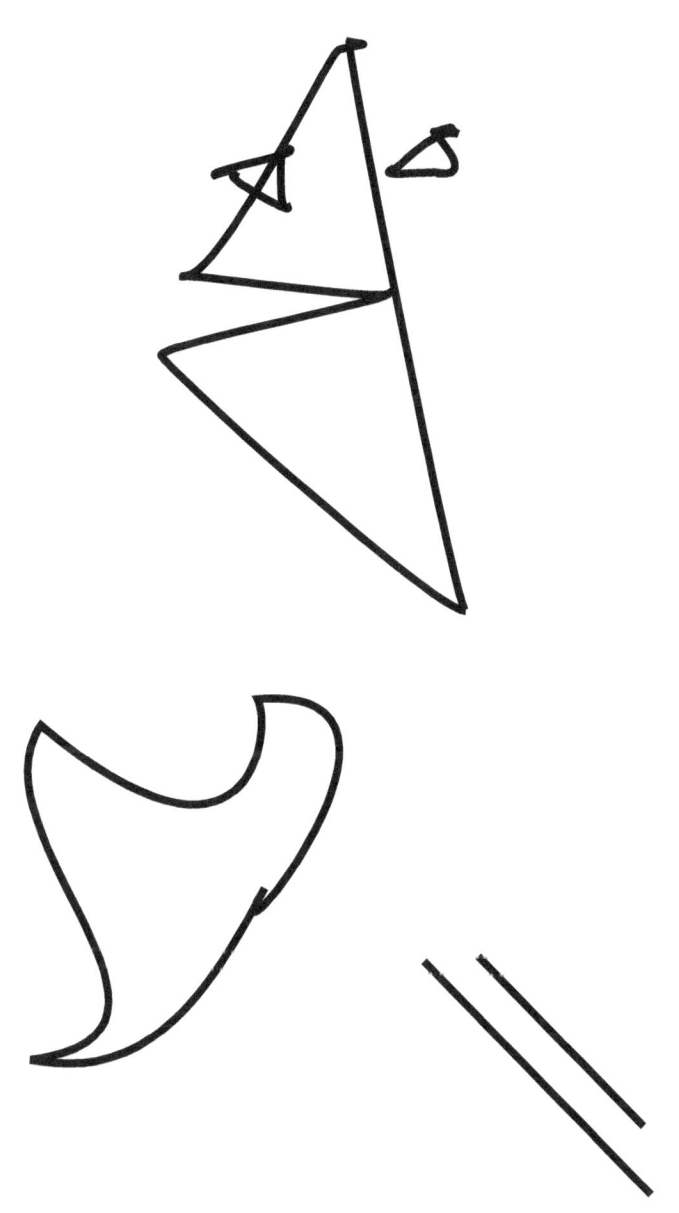

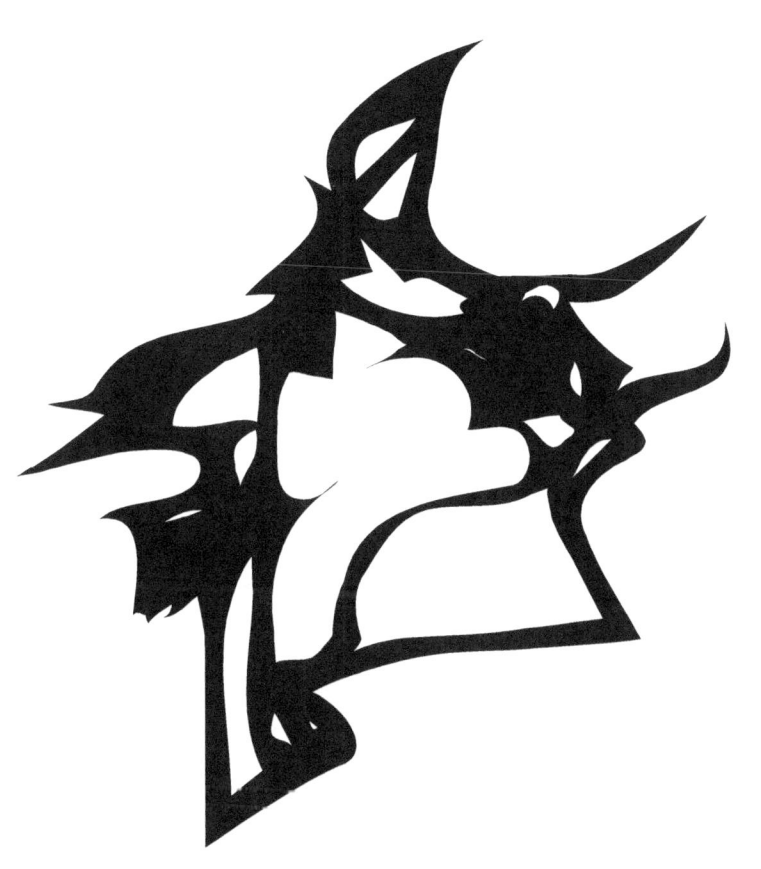

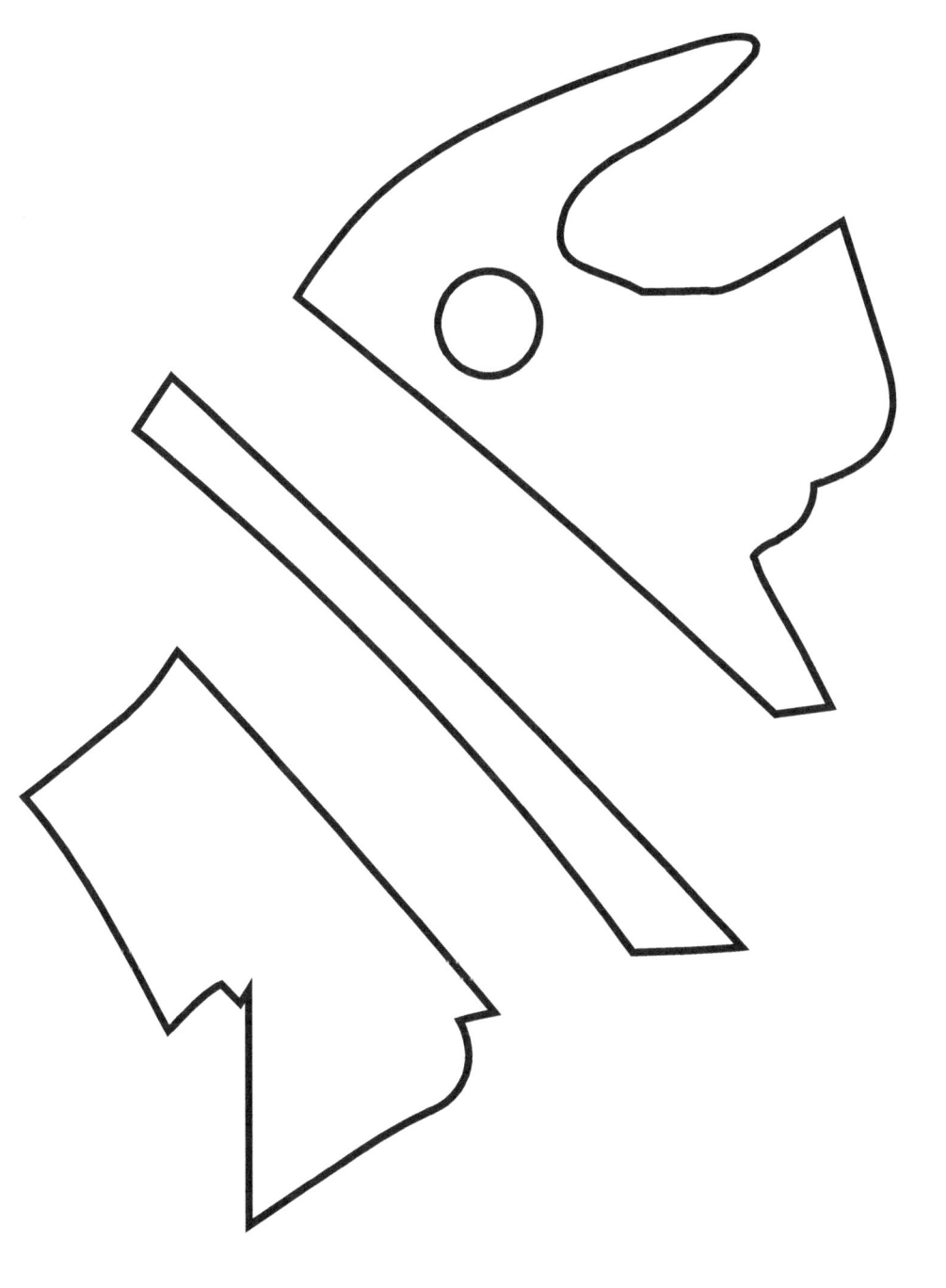

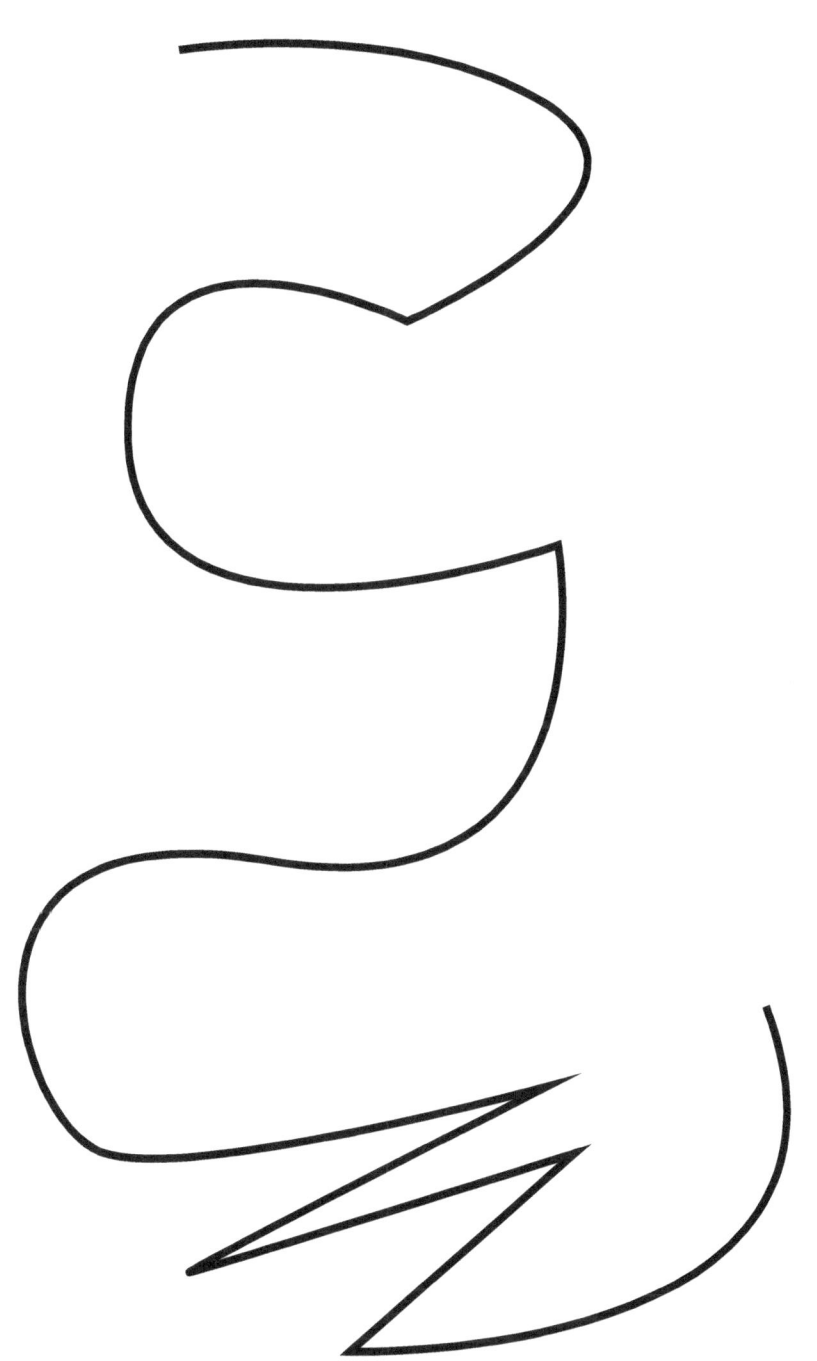

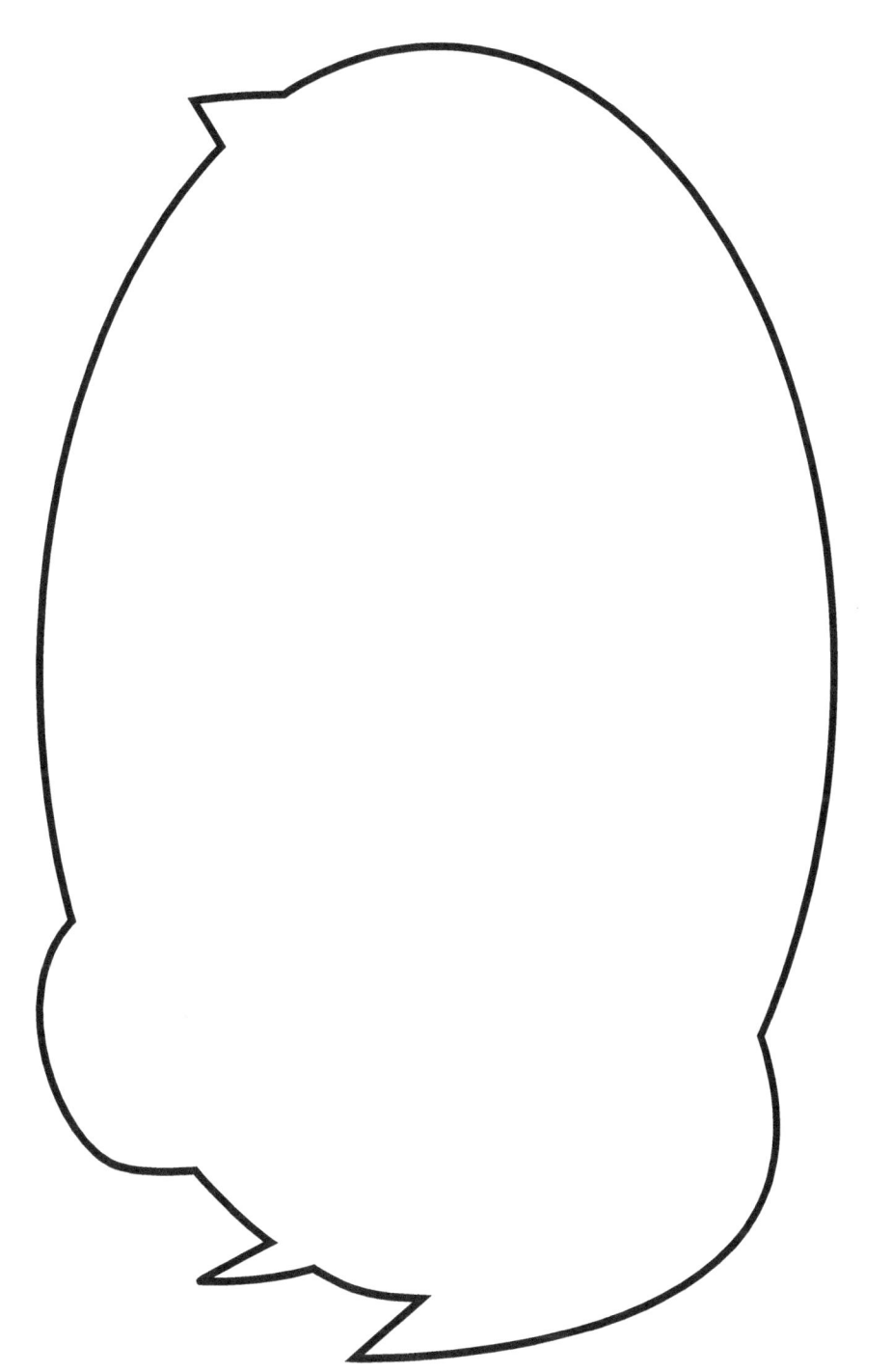

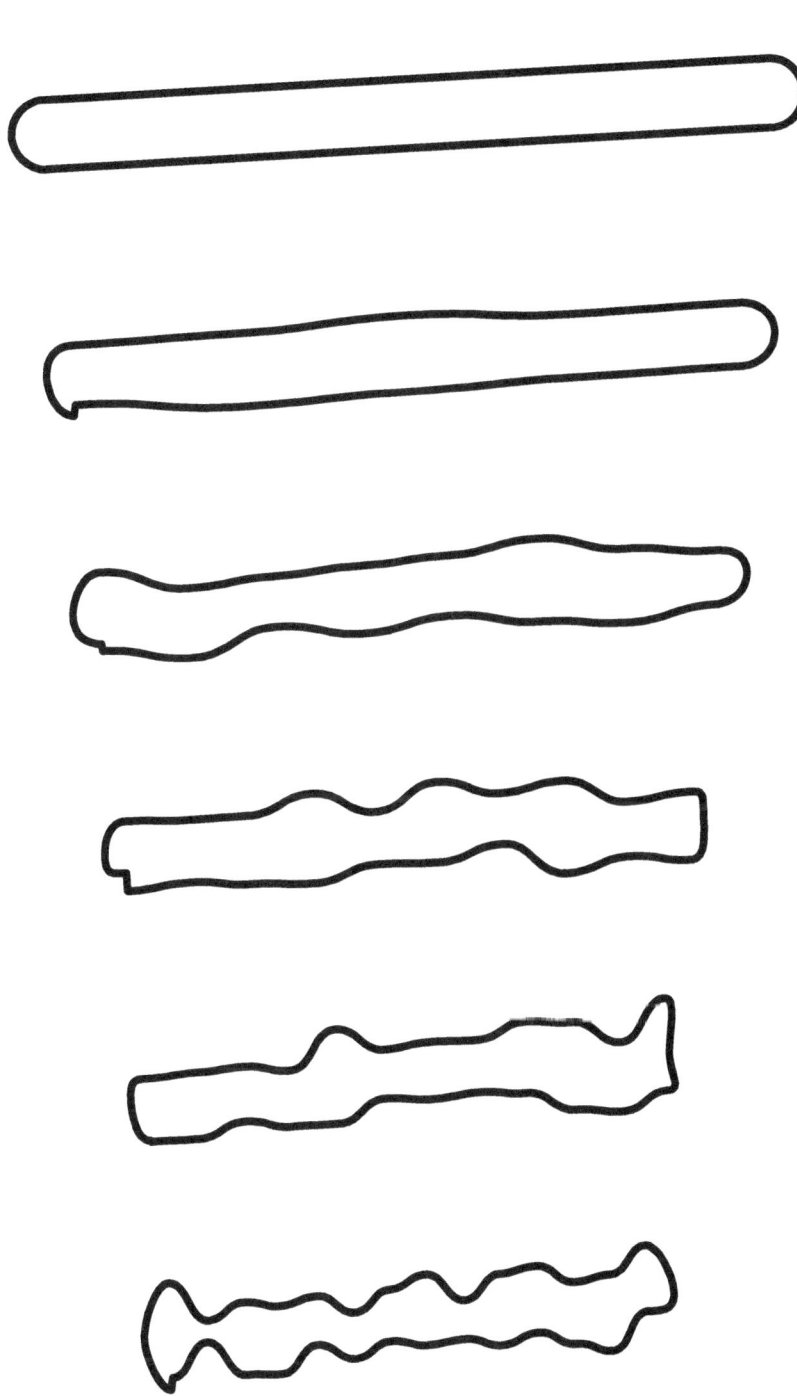

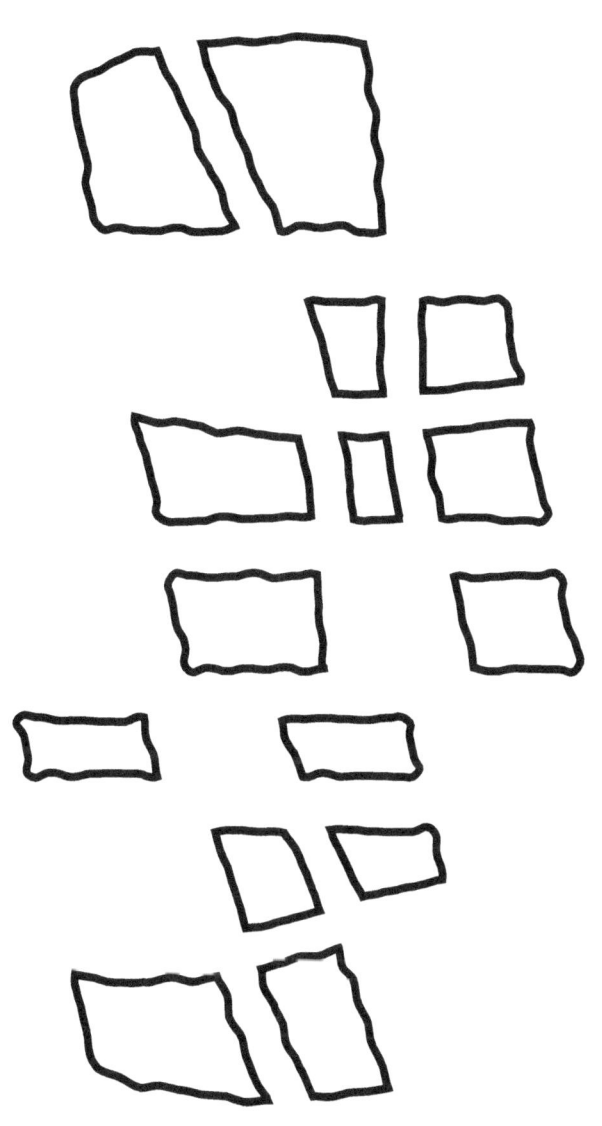